Kim,

I love

Bless &

revolution.

Dutty

Tried & True

Revelations of a Rebellious Youth

Dutty Bookman

BOOKMAN EXPRESS

Bookman Express, LLC
P.O. Box 31457
Washington, DC 20030-1457

BE@BookmanRising.com

ISBN: 978-0-615-52806-9
LCCN: 2011914795

Cover and photo illustrations by Aesthetics Now Design Agency.

LIVICATION

To the source of Life and all my blessings I offer this book,
which is a reality only through the will of the Universe.

And to every human who seeks within.

CONTENTS

PROLOGUE

Greetings in the name of all that is Creation. I am thankful that another person has opened this book. You are about to read a true story that I have wanted to tell for a fairly long time. Even before it was finished, I wanted to start telling it. What delayed its telling was, simply, the fact that it was not ready to be told. I waited patiently and started to wonder if I was really supposed to be the one to tell it. Time and Space have since shown me that I must tell this story, my story, because it is valuable and urgent, plus only I can tell it this way.

Ordinarily, less than three decades of life on Earth would hardly supply enough experience to warrant the need for a book such as this one. In my case though, I have lived my entire adult life in a conscious and purposeful way. My aim has historically been to expand my knowledge and sharpen my useful abilities, using both as my tools for making humble contributions to humanity. As such, I am not trying to be a writer or a communications professional, or to exist inside some other box in which people usually trap themselves in these times of mental slavery. I have become a career revolutionary and I am willing to do anything, within my capacity, that I perceive as a revolutionary step forward. At any given time, I can become a minister of government, an entrepreneur, a garbage collector or a street sweeper as long as I have determined that it is necessary for the revolution and that I am a suitable individual for that role.

At this point in time, I cannot say that I disregard violence and warfare as realities of this human era but I can truthfully declare that I find violence and warfare to be hindrances to human progress. I, myself, have no interest in shedding anyone else's blood or ending anyone else's life. Revolution is not always about guns and bombs or large groups of people protesting in the streets. Revolution involves being swift, effective and sometimes unexpected.

I have written these words, autobiographically, for the benefit of, at least, one person who may not even be born yet. I want

1

this person to know that wisdom accompanies the individual who fearlessly obeys the impulses within, especially when those impulses pose no foreseeable harm to others. The four years during which I proved this to myself – when it was proven to me via the forces of Creation – occurred between October 2006 and October 2010 on the Gregorian calendar. Therefore, this is the time period that informs the majority of this book. Recollections from any other period of time serve the purpose of adding relevant context to the main progression of the story.

My memory is a limited one in that it tends to recall feelings and emotions with much more ease than it remembers other details. For that reason, I am thankful for my journals in which I had meticulously written even the most trivial details of my experiences. The first major one is called the Black Book, with experiences recorded between May 11, 2006, while I was living in China, and July 6, 2007. The second is called the Career Book and it records my thoughts from August 10, 2007 to March 31, 2009. Those two journals are largely credited for providing the facts in this story. There is one other, called the Dragon Book; its exact contents are not required to adequately tell this story, although, as you will see, it is important to know that it exists.

In addition to the BB, CB and DB, I have other books that document different aspects of my chaotic process, which is scientific and artistic at once. They, and more sources, have been my fact-checking avenues as I set out to be as truthful as possible and to eliminate any fabrications, even partial ones, or exaggerations.

What you are about to read is really a long story, short. It is a chronicle outlining the challenges faced by a young man who genuinely wanted to increase social justice, and it tells of his advances and setbacks along the way. It is about a young man who self-actualized and discovered his role during a process of reconnecting with his indigenous culture. You will come to the realization that he tried his best to improve the human condition and he constantly sought the truth so that he could reflect it in turn. He tried to accomplish an ideal while staying true to himself.

As you read this man's story, know that he is I and any biases are my own. Accept my words in relation to your reality, for one man cannot know the fullness of this revolution with which we are all involved. I know what I need to know to do my task and so must you. Observe your signs keenly, interpret them wisely and follow them with the most positive intentions. I wish you many blessings along your journey.

Dutty Bookman.

2006
&
2007

1
RETURN OF THE UNKNOWN LEADER

October 3, 2006 is a date etched in my memory. It was the day I returned to Jamaica, my home from which I was exiled under the pretext of higher education. For six years I was a student at the Embry-Riddle Aeronautical University. Why? Because I had no career ambition after high school and my parents thought that I should go to college regardless, that's why. I had scanned through the degree programs and applied for Aerospace Engineering – seemingly the most challenging major – and I was accepted. Another Florida school accepted me but I wanted to experience the world famous Daytona Beach, which turned out to be nothing but the subject of overhyped marketing for tourism.

After two and a half years of studying "rocket science," I started going through an academic transformation. I switched programs to Software Engineering and toughed that out for another year, at which point I decided that I wanted to expel engineering from my life altogether. My social awareness was increasing and my refuge was ERAU's humanities department. I discovered a program called Aerospace Studies, a combination of a few core, aviation-related courses with the student's choice of three minors. I was quite happy about incorporating more social science courses into my weekly schedule and chose to pursue

Communication, International Relations and, since one minor was required to be technical, I went with Information Technology to complete the triumvirate of my quest to graduate. Of course, the drastic switch from engineering to humanities meant that a lot of the previous courses I did would no longer count towards my degree. Therefore I had to stay in school for more than the expected four years. At one point, I almost quit my studies out of frustration but my mother managed to persuade me to see it through to the end, even though I was already causing her financial strain.

Well, the end finally arrived in August 2006. I took about a month and a half to get my useful material possessions together and then I was on a plane to my beloved home. The stinking streets of Kingston were a breath of fresh air when I landed. I had been home most summers and Christmas seasons between semesters but I had been stuck in Florida for the final year or two for monetary reasons. So, there was a certain liberating and unmatched feeling associated with going home without a return ticket to the USA. I had so much that I wanted to accomplish. I was a young leader who had just broken my own shackles and was ready to spark a rebellion. Now, I could finally put my energy into activities of national empowerment and self-determination.

I was 23-years-old when I arrived, a month away from celebrating two dozen years on Earth. In fact, I spent the rest of 2006 doing two main things: partying hard and trying to gain weight. The result was a routine of eating dinner as prepared by my mother, going on the road to some party or other social gathering, then stopping at Manor Park, Red Hills Road or Liguanea for some pan chicken, depending on the direction I was coming from or where the crowd was going. Sometimes I had pan chicken left over to eat the next morning, sometimes I ate pan chicken before a party as well as after.

Besides that routine, I had another obsession — IdlerzLounge.com (known simply as IL). It was a website that I launched on July 11, 2000 out of a desire to be popular combined with my enthusiasm for HTML coding. I think that it was my passion for writing and ability to describe things vividly that led many Jamaican youths to become addicted to the website. The message board grew to be a unique community of intelligent, sarcastic, cynical and sensual young people. At its heights, most of the users formed cliques in Jamaica and South Florida and I mostly observed the phenomenon from my dorm room and, later, my off-campus apartment in Daytona Beach. I had a strange relationship with the members; many seemed to view me as an authority figure or otherwise different from them, even as I made every effort to erase any sense of such separation. In actuality, my obsession with IL grew just as theirs did. In my case though, I was embarked on a journey of scientific interpretation and manipulation. I was a social scientist in every sense of the term, and, in retrospect, I know that my attachment to IL at the time heavily influenced my decision to discard the possibility of a degree in engineering for something in the humanities. What I could not discard was the engineer's discipline and attention to detail. For example, in designing a passenger airplane or a rocket for space exploration, the tiniest error could mean instant death and destruction. Everything requires proper planning, lots of tests, data collection and patience. As I reflect on my young adulthood, I can safely say that I applied myself to all projects that I cared about like an engineer and IL was no different. In fact, since the site was the only thing that I completely controlled, I approached it more diligently than my schoolwork. I was so absorbed in the development of IL that my diet grew to be less than satisfactory as I often forgot to feed myself.

I was also heavily involved in the Caribbean Students Association (CSA) at school and I represented myself with all the Jamaican arrogance that generally made other islanders so weary. By 2002, I was elected Public Relations Officer for the statewide umbrella organization called the Florida Caribbean Students Association (FCSA). At the time, the support for FCSA was nowhere near its potential and that was evident based on the low attendance at its bi-annual conferences. My mandate was to help grow the membership of the FCSA and the major objective was to make the FCSA conferences the most anticipated events for as many Caribbean students in the state of Florida as possible. My main method was harnessing the communicative power of the internet and IL was the platform that largely contributed to my success. By 2004, when I finished serving the maximum allowed two terms in office, the conferences grew from about 200 to roughly 700 attendees. As far as I know, that was the fastest rate of growth in the organization's history.

I eventually campaigned to be the President of my local CSA. On election day, I lost by one vote, a defeat that did some damage to my confidence and forced me to start addressing my arrogance. I learned to observe myself more keenly in a bid to know myself better. All throughout that ordeal, I was going through a mental transformation, reading books of my own choosing, not just the ones assigned in school. The first book I can recall ever willingly reading was a biography of Ernesto 'Che' Guevara called *Che Guevara: A Revolutionary Life* by Jon Lee Anderson. It was the biggest and thickest book I ever read at the time, yet it was so enthralling that I read it day in and day out, finishing it much quicker than anticipated. Being exposed to so much of Guevara's journal entries, his raw thoughts in essence, I was impressed. Not only did his actions in life fascinate me, but even more exciting was the fact that he intentionally left behind his writings for the consumption of future generations. It was the greatest act of his ego and my ego found something to which it could relate. If I could not get my due recognition in one lifetime, I would get it in the next.

As a result of that kind of inspiration, the young man who returned to Jamaica was one with intense socialist rhetoric, especially as I interacted with my peers on IL. I knew within myself that I was not going to fail at whatever I made an effort to do, bearing in mind that I had no idea what I would do yet. Yes, I had plans and dreams but I was always ready to adapt as long as it led to meaningful change in my island nation. After Jamaica, I would go for the world. Even now, this basic truth of mine has not changed. What has changed is the quality of the energy that I have put into my effort, including the greater sense of humility that I am practicing to attain. Notably, I did not get to this point overnight but, rather, it was a non-stop process that took place throughout the years and it continues still. Most of that process can be discerned from the way I navigated amidst the memorable events of my life following my return to Jamaica.

2
RESONABLE PROPOSITION

On the Rock (that is, Jamaica), I naturally gravitated to my old high school friends. Some of us called ourselves the Canteen Crew, a name we adopted when we got to 6th Form – two optional years of high school that students enrolled in after getting their high school diplomas (essentially, grades 12 and 13). Students in 6th Form were allowed to drive to school and could leave the campus during breaks. Our school, Campion College, was a Jesuit-run, co-educational institution with the most outstanding academic reputation in the country. A lot of financially well-off families sent their kids to Campion and most students were accepted on the merit of their performance at the primary level. Most 6th Formers habitually ate their lunch off campus, at the Sovereign Center across Hope Road or elsewhere. We, in the Canteen Crew, were mostly inclined to eat at the school canteen, which was cheaper and allowed us to save our lunch money to get the latest Hip-hop CD's at the end of the week, or whatever else we desired in those days.

Ryan Strachan and Karsten 'Biggs' Johnson were among the first people I linked up with upon my return. They were not only Canteen Crew colleagues but also active IL members, and Strachan was Head Moderator, a decision-maker in the staff structure that I set up while living in Daytona Beach. Together,

Strachan and Biggs, along with a few other Idlerz (as IL members are still affectionately called to this day), were the ones who really helped me to recognize the reality of IL's evolution in Jamaica and, effectively, sent me back to the drawing board. They hardly knew what their jokes and comments did to my psyche – maybe they did – but their foresight was a treasure for me in that period of time when I was re-familiarizing myself with my own creation.

There was also Reggie Bell, a brother of mine in every aspect except by shared parentage. He was not only a Canteen Crew man but he was my fellow militant throughout many ordeals. We were in the same homeroom (along with André 'Froggy' Hall, Beauclaire 'Klipp' Leslie and others) when we started at Campion in 1st Form (7th grade). We lived in the same neighborhood and we both went to universities in Florida; he and Clint Beharry (who played a very significant role in establishing IL before his life journey led him elsewhere) visited me for a spring break holiday or two and I linked up with them at the University of Miami on some occasions. Reggie graduated in the expected timeframe and was already living and working in Jamaica by the time I returned. With his engineering degree, he found himself at the Radio Mona radio station on the campus of the University of the West Indies. By the time I got home, it had been renamed NewsTalk 93FM and, by the end of 2006, Reggie approached me with a proposition. He had caught wind of the station's need for new programming and he wondered if we could conceptualize a new radio show. I doubt that I hesitated for more than one second before accepting the offer.

At the start of 2007, Reggie and I met constantly for a month and a half. The usual venue for discussions was the attic in my Washington Boulevard home. That was my personal lab where I could find relative solitude under my mother's roof. It was truly a comfort zone for me and I often fell asleep up there. It was also the creative and productive space where Reggie and I put together a plan for a youth talk show called Reasoning. Reggie took our proposal to his supervisor at NewsTalk in mid-February and we simply waited after that.

3
MEET THY MAKER

As I was engaged in the hopeful process of being a radio personality, I was also starting to explore Jamaica's terrain more than I ever had before. My first major trip outside of Kingston happened in January 2007 with Reggie and a few other friends, including some well-seasoned hikers. We went to the Robin's Bay area in the parish of Saint Mary, where we parked the cars and started walking. It was very exciting to me and soon became a dangerous affair out of which my appreciation for life grew. The following account of that experience was written in the Black Book.

It was enjoyable, exhilarating, maybe a bit rejuvenating as well. About 2 hours of walking each way to and from a waterfall where we cooked and smoked and observed heavy rains transform serenity into a disaster zone. I was a little worried at some points during the downpour, especially when it became painfully obvious that the way we entered was impassable, but I had already suggested an alternative route over a fairly step hill that was clearly not intended for hiking... What got me reconsidering my stance on religion was Saturday's hike. When the heavy rain came down, the way we got around the most dangerous part of the river made me wonder if an almighty being was really watching us. I don't know if anybody else appreciated, as much as I did, the fact that a firmly rooted plant was perfectly angled for us to grab onto and pull ourselves up roughly 10 feet of relatively steep and surely slippery rock. That tree trunk, or whatever it was, was the key to our mobilization. It was just very uncanny how conveniently placed it was bearing in mind that area was not meant for hiking. [January 14, 2007, 10:36am, BB]

Even those words fail to do justice to the severity of the situation and the panic I felt as a result. There was a point in the whole ordeal when we all froze in awe of the rushing water preventing us from wading our way out of the dead end. None of the seven of us, including the seasoned hikers, had any clue how we would escape before the rising water level covered all areas of relative safety. It was at that point that I felt a gust of intuition convincing me to look up and to the left. I did it almost automatically and that was when I noticed the isolated plant that would become our saving grace. I shouted at Douglas and Peter (two of the experienced bushmen) and pointed at it. They approved and we all somehow found a way to grab unto it, and unto each other, until we got to more stable ground. Then we had to cut our way through thick overgrowth in order to get to calmer but still dangerous waters. In the end, we made it back to the vehicles and back to our respective homes.

When I got home that night and greeted my mother, I could not help but think about how she might have heard about my death on the evening news. Worse yet, my six friends and I could have been mysteriously missing, perhaps found lifeless a few weeks later or not at all. The experience signaled the beginning of a re-awakening for me; for the first time in my conscious life, I was aware of the presence of the active Universe. I felt and knew in my soul that Creation had a mission for me to fulfill for I was preserved to see another day.

4

FOR WANT OF MONEY

As February got underway, I was starting to feel the unwanted effects of unemployment. Despite the fact that I was being quite industrious, I was not quite plugged into the Jamaican economic system. I was building and working on my own advancement but I wasn't contributing to the financial profit of another person. That is to say that I didn't have a job. My mother was very concerned and became annoyed from time to time when she noticed how comfortable I appeared to be in a seemingly parasitic state. After all, she was feeding her 24-year-old college graduate and that was hardly what any parent of her generation expected. Of course, we the college-educated offspring (not to mention the members of my generation with less formal education) tended to be well aware of the hardships facing us during this phase of global neo-imperialist capitalism, but most parents simply did not grasp the fact. Those who happened to understand were largely in shock and, perhaps, could not come to terms with the reality of seeing such meager returns on their investment in a "good education" for their children.

Carrol (I sometimes like to call my mother by her first name, often with the intention to make her smile) was adamant – with words or body language – that I show some sign of caring about making it in the "real world," which was a grand imaginary world in my mind. Realizing that I was running out of money in my savings account to finance my pan chicken habit, I intensified my job search.

By the middle of the month, Reggie greeted me with the news that Dr. Anthony Abrahams – former government minister, host of the popular Breakfast Club radio program and part-owner of NewsTalk – showed an interest in putting Reasoning on air. I was elated, as I am sure Reggie was as well, although he was historically the calmer, less visibly moved individual between the two of us in times of pleasure and displeasure alike. As we entered into negotiations to determine the conditions and start date of the talk show, we also knew that it wasn't going to help us earn much until its popularity pulled corporate sponsorship or other advertising dollars. As meaningful as being on radio would be, I continued to search for other employment. Additionally, I had applied to a masters degree program in Government Studies at the University of the West Indies (UWI), Mona, and hoped to be accepted and enrolled in September. I got recommendations from two of my favorite Embry-Riddle professors to bolster the application. The first was Dr. Philip Jones who taught at the Arizona campus and met me in 2006 as a student in his Chinese history course when I was studying in China. The second was Dr. James Cunningham, who was my professor in Applied Cross-Cultural Communications, a course that I found very exciting. Even though recommendations were supposed to be delivered from the professors directly to the UWI admissions office, I was allowed to receive the recommendations from Dr. Jones and Dr. Cunningham in order to somehow expedite the process before an impending deadline. I therefore had the unique opportunity to read what they had to say about me and decided to record their words in my journal. First, Dr. Jones:

Gavin is an outstanding person. Intellectually, he stood out as the brightest of the 21 university students in the program... He has a thirst, a passion for knowledge, a searching and inquiring mind. His journal showed an unusual depth of insight... I have no doubt he will be a top student and, beyond that, make important contributions in his professional career. [January 30, 2007, 9:25pm, BB]

Incidentally, Dr. Jones is the only human being who was ever willingly given any of my major journals to read. As a part of his course, we had to keep a journal to record our experiences in China and I had brought the Black Book with me precisely because I intended to begin journaling my life experiences in China. When I learned of his assignment, I decided that I was not going to write two separate journals for the sake of protecting my innermost thoughts. Furthermore, I respected and trusted Dr. Jones almost as soon as I had my first conversation with him. Since I would probably never have to see him again after leaving China, I decided that it would be good to gain his feedback and wisdom by having him glimpse the products of my unusual mind. What I was unaware of was that, each year, he selected and announced what he thought to be the top three journals from that group of students. He typically never told the students until the day he returned the journals, and so it was that on the last day of class, as he returned ours to us, that he declared me the blue ribbon winner for first place. His wife, Dr. Chen (who was our Mandarin language teacher while there), spoke to me privately that day. I cannot forget the huge smile on her face as she told me how impressed her husband was when he read my thoughts the previous evening. It was as though she had never seen him like that before. That must have been the moment when I discovered the truly powerful effect of my writing and, ever since, I relentlessly continued to record my experiences and related thoughts.

Dr. Cunningham, who was also the husband of another of my favorite professors (Mrs. Cunningham taught me Information Technology courses), had the following words to contribute to my bid for enrollment at UWI.

Gavin was one of the brightest students I had in my Applied Cross Cultural Communications class... His character, intellectual insight and positive disposition is solid; Gavin is a mature and balanced young man... He is bright, personable, confident in his responses – and a very good writer. I believe him when he says that his heart is set on earning a graduate degree in Governmental Studies at UWI. [January 30, 2007, 9:25pm, BB]

I really did have my heart set on it. I had spent hours going through the UWI catalog to determine which program was right for my personality and aspirations. I genuinely thought that I would have put all my energy into that Government Studies program. It was not to be though. By May, I learned that I was not accepted to the program. In the meantime, I was earning money.

5

THE PLANTATION STILL EXISTS

One day in the middle of March, my mother told me that she had a feeling that I got a job. I got a phone call that same day from the manager at Monte Carlo Gaming, a lounge and bar that resembles a casino but is not legally referred to as one because there are no humans administering the games; everything was machine-based and so it was a "gaming lounge." For most intents and purposes though, I call it a casino and it was located on the same property as the Terra Nova Hotel on Waterloo Avenue.

The lady who called, and who I later met for an interview, went by the last name of Melhado, a family name speculated to be among "the 21 families" of Jamaica that worked for or against the responsible development of the nation's economy, depending on who you ask. About three days later, March 16, with maybe $500 (approximately US$5) remaining in my bank account, I began working there as a supervisor. I was about to get a fast lesson in the reality of a 21st century plantation... and I was not about to become the model house Negro. On April 8, I wrote:

I am not sure how much longer I can tolerate this occupation. The feeling of slavery doesn't seem to subside. I can see that experience and seniority doesn't mean much to management/owner(s), judging by the mentality of all staff in general. This is capitalism at its prime. Efficiency at the cost of humane treatment. At present, I am Gavin Hutchinson, the cog in the machine of sin... Apparently this is how the system is set up. Funny how no one explained anything to me and no contract was signed or anything. Monkey business. [April 8, 2007, 1:00am, BB]

I was very keen to learn about the underlying cause of all the symptoms I observed. I soon grew to despise a certain surname, Hussey, which represented another family of the "plantocracy" that counted the casino and the hotel among its assets. After brief investigations, I happened upon information suggesting that they still owned a plantation somewhere in the country and continued to profit handsomely in post-colonial Jamaica. I also learned about a widespread speculation of the patriarch's past connection to the marijuana trade. I certainly had no qualms about marijuana but I wondered why the relevant authorities, knowingly, would not have charged him for trafficking in illegal substances, meanwhile people distributing or possessing minute quantities of the herb were incarcerated daily. In my mind, this man, his family and the other twenty families like his were quite possibly a cancerous legion that sucked the life out of hardworking Jamaicans. I was pretty much ready to form a union.

As the days went by, I grew to appreciate why my fellow employees at Monte Carlo tolerated the clear injustices, the oppressive regulations and the underhanded tactics of the employers (all represented by the face of Miss Melhado, which was beautiful yet despicable). Many of us had never seen so much money before. We were paid weekly and we were paid in cash. It was a great feeling to open one of those envelopes every seven days, plus some of us were supporting children, paying bills and otherwise trying to stay afloat amidst the chaos of the system. I was probably the least stressed in this respect. I lived with my mother, I borrowed her car or took the bus from a relatively short distance away and I had no children to care for. I had the luxury to think about my career path and more time at my disposal to develop myself, which was more than a majority of hostesses, cashiers and even fellow supervisors could say for themselves. I certainly counted my blessings but I was also livid at the state of things and I wanted widespread rebellion. My fire intensified when I took note of some of the characters that frequently patronized the establishment. Politicians, including one who became a government minister after the next election, were among the avid horseracing and roulette players. Even an ambassador from another Caribbean nation was frequently spotted playing slots in the middle of the day. Some of them spent so much time there that I sincerely wondered when they found the time to attend to national affairs. If they didn't care about national service then did they, at least, consider the retention of their jobs to be of any importance? Was it that the probability of winning money at Monte Carlo proved less risky than relying on their consistent monthly incomes? I was perplexed for a while. Soon, one politician demonstrated the level of desperation, greed and corruption that drove most, if not all politicians in my view. This particular man, according to my written account, *"stole money from the establishment. First he tried to reclaim $40, U.S., that he had bet and lost on a roulette table. I witnessed this first-hand. Then, as I was told by a young lady who works with me, he received $400 (U.S.) credit on his roulette station through an error by the cashier. He did not seek to rectify the situation, but instead he cashed it out and told the young lady to put it on another table. Apparently, he bet it all away, not winning anything, but he is still a common criminal in my eyes."* [May 9, 2007, 2:12pm BB]

On the day when I wrote that, I also signed up for a writing course to be instructed by John Maxwell, whose weekly column had quickly become my favorite feature in the Sunday Observer. I gladly paid the $10,000 for the chance to meet him and learn from his wisdom.

In the final hours of May, I submitted two important requests to upper management at Monte Carlo. The first was that I not be scheduled for anymore Wednesday night shifts because Reasoning was about to debut on June 6 and our agreement with the station was that we would air from 10:30pm to 11:30pm weekly. The second request was that I be allowed four consecutive Saturday mornings to attend John Maxwell's class as of June 9. I knew that either one of the requests might rub them the wrong way, but to ask both at the same time was comparable to being suicidal. The fact was that they were both urgent matters so I had little choice. Two days later, the first day of June, I received my answer as soon as I stepped through the door for the morning shift. Melhado made it a point of duty to make an example out of me, loudly letting me know that, regarding Maxwell's class, "everybody knows" that Monte Carlo staff were not allowed to go to school. The obvious interpretation based on her words and her tone was that the company culture did not encourage personal development. Employees were indeed slaves and the employers were proud of their slave-driving techniques with refined efficiency throughout the generations. Turning to the matter of the radio show, I reminded her of the day when she interviewed me for the job and that, in no uncertain terms, I informed her that I may have to juggle Monte Carlo work with other projects that I was working on. Well, she conveniently forgot about that and fired back by letting me know that I was free to resign and go home. I laughed and went about my work for the day.

Two days after that, I walked into public embarrassment again. This time, printed photographs of me in violation of ridiculous rules were mounted on a wall. We were not supposed to lean against a wall or speak to each other during our 9-hour shifts; for eight hours we were supposed to stand straight up or walk around aimlessly until a task was required of us, and during our lunch hour (which was never enough to combat the pain or fatigue) we had to go directly to a small, dilapidated lunchroom. We weren't allowed to use our cell phones unless we went into our cars in the parking lot (those who had cars) and our restrooms might as well had been sties. I realize that a lot of it was a norm and that some workers in many parts of the world suffered worse tribulations, but the inequality irked me like nothing else. If I saw Melhado or any Hussey use the same restroom or eat lunch in the area designated for us, I would have been satisfied.

The night after the incident with the pictures, I decided that it was a good time to take Melhado up on her offer. At my appointed break time, I clocked out for the last time, knowing well that, in 1838, the plantations were not abolished along with slavery.

6

HOLDING A MEDZ ON THE AIRWAVES

---

*The morning after... I could use a morning-after-pill as I feel pregnant with
dissatisfaction. The show was not bad at all, but it could have been so much
better. I could have been so much better as a host.* [June 7, 2007,
10:04am, BB]

Above is an effective summary of my relationship with
Reasoning for the first few months. I was always trying to figure
out how to improve myself, having neither formal journalistic
education nor prior traditional media experience. I was running
purely on the confidence afforded me through my leadership on
IdlerzLounge.com; my convictions were additional fuel.

Our first episode's official guest was John Maxwell, three days
before he and I would meet in person. I remember how happy I
was to have such a stalwart associated with the launch of the
program. Only if I suffered head trauma and related memory loss
could that feeling ever be taken away from me.

Two days later, Reggie and I met Mrs. Jacqueline Lynch-
Stewart, general manager for the Bob Marley Foundation. The
meeting took place in her office on the grounds of the Bob
Marley Museum and, after about eighty minutes of conversation,
we became fast friends. I told her that I was in need of a job and
she promised to keep me in mind. In the meantime, my existence

revolved around the Reasoning routine. Between the typical Thursday and the following Sunday, the main priority was to conceptualize the next week's episode, not that Reggie and I were losing sleep over it but we were very devoted and highly motivated. We wanted each episode to be as meaningful and relevant as possible. In fact, we often joked that we didn't have much time to build the brand because we were sure to be discovered as rebels. So it was with an impending dismissal in mind that we bolstered each hour of programming with serious preparation. By Monday or Tuesday, we would begin doing outreach to get the needed young panelists in the studio, as well as the appropriate special guests for the subject matter. We researched for facts that would either support or refute our opinions – we made every attempt to be objective while not hiding our individual biases. We sometimes conducted quick polls, through IL or otherwise, and we usually kept busy until Wednesday evening. Then, there would be a sort of calm before the storm. Barring any unforeseen incidents that caused us to drive around or make anxious phone calls, we would sit outside the NewsTalk building and just absorb the calm energy of the UWI campus. In retrospect, I loved those moments the most, with just one hour or so to go before show time. My mind was often projecting into the future, knowing the planned progression of the show and also knowing that I was going to be granted a few more minutes to express myself freely to a national audience. That energy would build up and then I would get nervous, sometimes visible and uncontrollably nervous. But then, Reggie would position himself in front of the board and cue our theme song. Then, I would know that in another 45 seconds or so, I would have to shake off the nerves and say something... and it could be anything at all that I wanted to say. What liberation! Each week that I spoke, the understood, expanded translation of whatever I said was, *"This is Gavin 'Dutty' Hutchinson, a rebellious youth in the midst of Babylon! I somehow got to a position where you can hear me live on your radio and, until I'm discovered, I'll be kicking in the door and saying whatever I feel needs to be said."* That moment, at about 10:31pm, was the climatic moment for me and I would then proceed to bear my soul out to humanity by the end of the show. The Reasoning routine would reset itself shortly after 11:30pm, after Reggie and I discussed our initial feelings and criticisms about that particular episode. The next day, Thursday again, we would be giving each other more suggestions about how we thought we could improve the quality of the program.

We were also constantly in the streets, hanging out in places that many of our peers dared to observe only in passing. We constantly travelled by bus or robot taxi, sometimes walking, especially when my mother discovered a bag of herbs in her car and banned me from driving it indefinitely (mercifully, she allowed me to use it to go to the station on Wednesday nights). The result was that we were more connected to the everyman of Jamaica than we had ever been. Our mission was to use the intellectual benefits of our education, the few resources at our disposal and our unique platform to stimulate more Jamaicans to understand each other as well as understand the state of things globally. We felt like Jamaica was ripe for it and we worked to harvest other young minds before they rot.

Before the second episode, UWI had responded to my graduate school application with the unfortunate news that I was not accepted. I remember feeling like that was an unfortunate decision for UWI, and resolving to put all my intellectual energy into making Reasoning count for the benefit of Jamaica.

7
AMISTAD AND FRIENDS, RED, RED, RED

Red Stripe, arguably the most popular beer in Jamaica, has ridden too high on its horse. Members of IL are angered by a piece in the 'Red Hot Jamaica' magazine, published by Robinson Entertainment Media. Racist statements were made, and IL members are on top of it. I am truly proud. I have jumped on the bandwagon to shake up the establishment with letters to the media giants as well as to Diageo, the parent company for Red Stripe and just about every liquor brand in Jamaica. [August 10, 2007, 11:30am, CB]

My very first entry in the Career Book recorded my thoughts at the dawn of my campaign against Diageo. My heart was waiting for the enemies of the people to expose themselves and it seemed like I emerged onto the radio landscape at the right time. The described article was printed in an official magazine meant to promote the Red Stripe brand for the summer party season. In it, there were blatant allusions to dark-skinned people as inferior, including one striking phrase, "Amistad and friends." Knowing that there was a slave ship called "Amistad" (dramatized by a popular film of the same name), many young people found it offensive and the charge was led on the internet, especially via Facebook, and certainly boosted by the galvanized Idlerz. Months before, I had introduced a discussion area on the message board to facilitate more serious discussion than the prevalent norm; the Red Stripe saga brought added activity to that area. It didn't take long for Reggie to agree that Reasoning had a duty to amplify the collective voice calling for Diageo to publicly accept responsibility for their oversight in authorizing the distribution of the magazine, and for the disrespect thus shown. We launched our own investigation.

In a short time, we discovered who wrote the article; it was somebody who we knew. We determined that the article was written in jest, perhaps common uptown humor that evolved throughout the generations from the humor of slave masters. Who knows... but the author seemingly did not intend to offend anyone. Therefore, we put the blame squarely on the shoulders of the company's marketing manager, whose photograph and personal message emblazoned the first page of the magazine. Very soon, he responded to letters from Idlerz with a letter of his own, privately. I, and others, didn't feel satisfied. I went to town (so to speak) with Red Stripe on the air and off. At any reasonable opportunity, I reminded our listeners about the situation and constantly implied the fact that the people had the power to affect the future of the brand. I was well aware that our listenership was nothing compared to a daytime program on any of the more popular stations among the youth demographic and that made me blaze my fire even hotter. If only ten young people would hear me for the rest of time, I was going to make sure that all ten of them would grasp the severity of the situation. Neither eight nor nine of them would satisfy me; I was aiming for maximum impact.

I would soon reliably learn that our efforts were being recognized within the ranks at Diageo and that it was causing them some discomfort. I always wondered if IL or Reasoning or even my name ever appeared in official correspondences or records within the Red Stripe organization. That surely would have done wonders for my confidence and my ego, no doubt. Either way, I was happy about the unofficial scoop and I was motivated to maintain my intensity for as long as it would take.

Thankfully (mainly from the perspective of Red Stripe), an article appeared in the first Sunday Observer of September. It included a public acknowledgement and apology issued by the marketing manager. The thinking youth of Jamaica thought that was a better approach by him.

During August, we chose to have a multi-part discussion about the general elections; the exception was August 22 when we spoke, mostly, about the aftermath of Hurricane Dean, which had just done major damage to some rural parts of the nation. The details of those political discussions have largely been forgotten because I was hardly inspired by the end of them. We even had an episode where two leaders of the youth parties were bickering so wildly that I was happy to let them argue out of control and unmediated so that we could record it for the ages, for future generations to see the pointlessness of partisan politics. My enthusiasm returned in September when we aired our two-part series on classism in Jamaica, inspired by the Red Stripe saga. The producers of Reasoning – one Reggie and one Dutty – were not content to let the issue fall by the wayside because the beer company issued an apology. It was more than just an opportunity to expel some of the excess energy of our youth but also a chance to discuss the deeper cultural issues at hand. We sought to effect a positive change in the very core of the Jamaican way of life.

We're going to leave a big impression between now and the end of the year, provided we remain on air. [August 24, 2007, 2:07am, CB]

8
DON'T STOP

As Reasoning continued to improve, I was also working on changes to IL. Karelle Samuda, an Idler living in the Washington, DC area, resurrected an idea that I relished instantly. She had just taken over the position of Head Moderator, after the resignation of Strachan, and she wanted us to pursue the addition of blogs to the website. The writer in me supported the notion and I somehow found US$309.00 to acquire the software that I liked, including the blog add-on and a new photo gallery. Since IL's staff consisted of volunteers, and I had difficulty getting Ryan 'Smitty' Smith to find the time to install the new software, I ended up spending hours upon hours working on it (with Smitty playing an advisory role) until I re-opened IL Forumz (the message board) about a week and a half later. It was a highly frustrating experience for me, especially coupled with the fact that I was intensifying my job hunt again. An October 17 journal entry summed up my mood at the time:

A high level of frustration has taken root within me today. One factor is that IL's re-opened message board has been dissatisfactory (or unsatisfactory?). A lot of errors are emerging, and a lot of ungrateful members are emerging as well. Times like these, I feel ready to throw in the towel. Ironic it is that I told all staff to exercise patience, yet my impatience is overcoming me...

Financially, I am not doing too well... I wonder if my priorities are wrong for believing so much, and investing so much, in my long term goals? What is clear to me is that I need a job immediately. I'm making my life miserable unnecessarily. [October 17, 2007, 2:43am, CB]

Stress crept up on me from all angles. Before October was done, I had lost enough money to a brief addiction to playing poker, plus my mother also reminded me of my debt to her for losing a lot of money when I staged an IL anniversary party called *I-20*. The first time I threw that party with Brian 'Capo' Campbell, we profited modestly. That was in 2003 at the, then, new hotspot known as Weekenz. The party brand itself became an instant legend among Idlerz and we knew that we were in good position to profit more handsomely the following year. So, in the 2004 summer season, we gained the support of HYPE TV and my mother took a risk by investing a large sum of money. I was also in talks with a brethren named David Mullings, an Idler who had recently formed his own website, including a message board with some similarities to IL. I had actually offered my assistance to him in the early stages of his venture and his brand, RealVibes.net was becoming a household name. He was very enthusiastic about sponsoring *I-20* through his work with Jamaica National and I was very trusting of him. Very soon though, the relationship went sour and the major sponsorship that I was expecting did not happen. It took me years since then to experience a feeling of forgiveness at the thought of his name. The other unfortunate thing that occurred was that another, more popular promoter staged a party across the street from our venue, Backyaad, another new hotspot that we discovered. His party offered the same benefits as *I-20* but at half the price! After weeks of promoting on HYPE TV and creating a buzz around *I-20*, the more experienced man simply leveraged his economies of scale and, in what seemed like one week, prepared an event of his own so that people who parked in the main parking lot would see his party first as they walked towards Backyaad. Our crowd was decent, but mostly consisted of Idlerz and friends of me and Capo. All our excess advertising amounted to next to naught. My mother paid the price when the negative balance was revealed at the end of the night. She rekindled my guilt and shame over three years later when, in 2007, she informed me that she had just paid off the associated debt on her credit card. A heart condition that I had was soon active again and, that year, I cried tears of sorrow on my birthday.

Actually, I did not put on another anniversary party until July 2007, and it was at a less extravagant scale. It was a house party called *Lucky 7*, a name I found fitting because, apart from the fact that it was held on a "Friday the thirteenth" (a superstitiously bad lucked day), it was IL's 7th anniversary and I was also beginning to feel good fortune associated with the recent launch of Reasoning plus the changes I was enacting on IL. It was kept at the home of an Idler on Roehampton Drive and people contributed the beverages. It was just Idlerz and close friends and it was a very happy time for me. It was the first IL party where I was not constantly running around and attending to various matters. It was much less work and much more connecting with the people who supported my pet project and helped it become not only one of the first, but also one of Jamaica's most popular, award-winning websites. I was also proud of myself for not buying too much into the prevalent hype of the Kingston scene and maintaining a level of humility and homeliness in the community that I nurtured.

One of the persons who stood out to me was a longtime acquaintance from Campion College. His name was Taiwo McKenzie and on IL he was known as Tarrentino. Our initial connection was as teammates on the high school basketball team. We had the typical small talk at *Lucky 7* but I had sensed a greater wisdom in him than I had expected. On another day after that, we had a conversation online. He asked me what my goals were with IL and it led to me sharing my general aspirations with him. I remember that I was unusually open about my plans, as I had become a secretive individual by this time, but I just had a great appreciation for his energy. After I told him an epistle, he returned to me some of the nicest words of encouragement and offered to support me in any way that he could. Then, as we were concluding our conversation, Taiwo typed to me, "... don't stop..."

I would never speak to him again. In November 2007, I was in Florida for a few days and I received the tragic news that Taiwo and his girlfriend were kidnapped and brutally slain. I never spoke to him again, yet his last words to me became amplified. After his funeral service, I sat petrified for a long time and then cried when I thought that everybody had left the church:

At Taiwo's funeral this morning, I was in a deep reflection about my task... my duty to Jamaica. By the time they were accepting open tributes, I wanted to get up and tell the entire congregation of my dedication to rid this country of the evil. I wanted to ignite a fire in all other young people there, and I couldn't. I sat still... I made the speech in my head. The pastor ended up saying everything I wanted to say, but with the assistance of the scripture. It struck such a chord with me that, by the time the service was over, I was unable to hold back my tears any longer. He asked, "Who will pick up the mantle!?"

I wanted to shout out, then and there, "Me!" My shame held my tongue. This was a time for Taiwo. I highly doubt that shame will be a factor in the future. [November 19, 2007, 6:22pm, CB]

2008

9

THE WAY FORWARD

As the figurative curtains descended on the year 2007, I was pleasantly surprised by Mrs. Stewart, who offered me a job at 56 Hope Road. The same December day that I met with her to finalize the contract, I also got my hair twisted at Jus Natural Hair Studio, which was then located on the Museum grounds. Those twists would become the dreadlocks to adorn my head years later. By the end of my first week on the job, I was already overwhelmed with lots of work and not that much in salary. I was constantly thankful though, for it was a much more uplifting environment than that at Monte Carlo.

The general nature of my job was to assist in making the celebrations for Bob Marley's 63rd Earthday a reality and a success. I was off to a terrible start. I barely had the chance to settle in before a barrage of tasks was being thrown at me. Mrs. Stewart and her assistant, plus Mrs. Rita Marley and her assistant, and even another lady emailing me from another country, all found in me a person eager to share their burdens. The result was that I felt like I was carrying the heaviest load; it was the weight of the tasks compounded with the suddenness that really knocked me off balance. It was as though a drum set, a bass guitar and Bob Marley's Gibson Les Paul electric guitar were all dropped from the top of a very high building and I was supposed to catch them all, set them down carefully and then play 'One Love' all by myself. I was simply not up to the task and it didn't take long for Mrs. Marley to get upset.

After some discussions about what was expected of me, I transitioned into an office manager for the *Africa Unite – Smile Jamaica 2008* office, which I helped to set up. My main project was the coordination of the *Africa Unite Youth Symposium* and I was excited as my last entry of 2007 shows:

2008 will probably start off with 2 months of joyful stress. These next 8 weeks or so should be pivotal to my life's direction. I am eager to witness what will unfold... [December 31, 2007, 3:27am, CB]

Well, what unfolded were not quite eight weeks of joyful stress, but more like five or six; and it was a very exciting time for me. The work was, indeed, fast-paced and often taxing but the energy cultivated inside those high walls at 56 Hope Road was unlike anything I knew before. For all my perceived suffering and stress only months before, and a still deteriorating relationship with my mother who was a breath away from disallowing me to live in her home due to our differences, the Museum was my refuge. There, my spirit was constantly lifted, discounting the occasional bouts of office politics that I would sometimes inadvertently get drawn into.

Another source of light in my life was the fact that NewsTalk extended our program's timeslot each week to an hour and a half. Given the fact that we were such media outlaws and outcasts at the time, this was seen as approval and validation of the quality of our service. We wanted to boost the momentum by airing an episode with Damian 'Jr. Gong' Marley and Stephen 'Raggamuffin' Marley as special guests. I had proposed *The Black Series* to Reggie as our way of commemorating Black History Month on Reasoning, and I thought they would have been great additions to the ongoing discussion. With that decided, I took the opportunity to approach Damian one day at the steps to the Ghetto Youths International office. He was "very receptive," according to my January 21 entry in the Career Book, but I first had to run it by Steve. That didn't surprise me because it was already obvious to me that the decision-maker was usually Raggamuffin and I appreciated the order. I found him the next day and he was hardly in the mood that I hoped he would be in; he said that he wanted to listen to the show first before making a decision. Another two days later, I asked him if they had a chance to listen to the last episode and he said no. I was disappointed but equally glad because that episode was one of our discussions about intimate relationships between men and women, which we occasionally did to attract more young people to our brand. I didn't want Robert Nesta Marley's sons' first impression to be that our program had no revolutionary substance.

In the end, they did not appear on Reasoning, which highly disappointed me. On our very first episode on June 6, 2007, the very first thing that we did as the show's theme song faded out was to play Jr. Gong's song, 'Confrontation,' from beginning to end. Only after that did the Jamaican public hear our voices for the first time. The spirit and message of that song was the driving force of Reasoning, which was fitting because the 'Welcome To Jamrock' album was catalytic to the revolutionary vibrations of me, Reggie and so many other of Jamaica's young people.

For the majority of my contracted time at 56 Hope Road, I worked hard to make the *Africa Unite Youth Symposium* a reality. When my weaknesses were exposed early in the process, a lady by the name of Carleene Samuels was brought on board to lead the charge and I was relegated to a supporting role, which was quite fine by me. Carleene, who, I would later learn, was the mother of one of David 'Ziggy' Marley's daughters, brought along a bright and beautiful young assistant by the name of Lesley-Ann Welsh. She was an ex-Campionite like myself, about three years younger in age, but certainly my intellectual counterpart in many respects. We became great friends on the job and, by the time the Symposium began, Carleene blended into the background and allowed us to take charge of the event. It was a very empowering experience for me as the following journal excerpts indicate:

Today got off to a shaky start, but the Youth Symposium went well. Unfortunately, the turnout was scanty; nevertheless, the quality was good. The speeches were relevant and the discussions stimulated my mind. I was able to get in a few key words that seemed to have commanded respect. By the end of the evening, a young man called Che from Canada approached me with the possibility of attending a similar function in Toronto. [February 4, 2008, 11:11pm, CB]

The young man was Che Kothari, instigator and executive director of Manifesto Community Projects. Little did I know about his persistence at the time but that would soon become apparent. The following day's highlight for me was a speech given by Mutabaruka. I relished the chance to speak with him, so much so that I did not realize that another person who I met that day could later have a great impact on my life.

The Symposium was great today... Reggie and I reasoned with a lady named Mama G... a maroon. She has offered to take us hiking/camping in the hills. I am excited about doing that. [February 5, 2008, 11:48pm, CB]

On the third and final day of the Symposium, I had my crowning moment. I had known since January 29 that I was going to be a speaker on the final day, and I was very excited about the fact, but I had no idea what I was going to say. So, I decided to carefully analyze the various points of view expressed over the first two days of the Symposium, and it was on the night of February 5 that I went into the attic at home and worked on it. I awoke and completed it in the morning before heading over to the Symposium's venue, Liberty Hall, which was founded by Jamaica's first national hero, Marcus Mosiah Garvey. In front of a modest crowd, I delivered a speech that summarized how I thought pan-African youth should move forward in unity.[*]

---

[*] See page 151 for the full text of my speech.

On Bob's birthday I delivered a speech at about quarter to eleven in the morning. I don't know how I did it, but it was well received and I got to vent. 'The Way Forward' was what I named it, and I believe it stimulated constructive, solution-oriented discussion at the Symposium. [February 7, 2008, 12:55am, CB]

Still reflecting on yesterday. After my speech, a very verbose and eloquent (and knowledgeable) old man – a Reverend – delivered to me a message from God. He looked me square in the eyes and told me I will be responsible for my generation (paraphrase). I took it, and still take it quite seriously. After all, this was an atmosphere of militancy and urgency...
Afterwards, Mama G approached me for a copy of my speech. I gave her the one I had. That was flattering. Again still, Che came up to me to say that I am "definitely coming to Toronto." He had obviously resolved this within himself during my speech. [February 7, 2008, 7:37am, CB]

On the 7th, we brought the youth delegates, who were all or mostly from other Caribbean countries, to Nine Mile, Saint Ann, the birthplace of Bob Marley. It was my first time there and it was a wonderful experience. Lesley was in charge and I played a supporting role; Che came along with us. That day signaled the completion of my major responsibility for the Bob Marley Foundation but also the beginning of a new project. Like I said, Che came along with us...

10
RECALIBRATING MY LIVITY

Our trip to Nine Mile revealed a shameful reality to us. The residents of the community were not reaping adequate benefits from its association with Bob Marley's name. For instance, the Stepney All Age School, where Bob Marley himself attended, was not in the best condition. The climatic moment was when we were at the end of our tour of the Bob Marley Mausoleum and we saw a boy's arm reach under a large, locked gate from the street. He was begging us for money. Che, Lesley and I were flabbergasted. It didn't take long for Che's spirit of resolve and persistence to be revealed. He was going to find a way to assist this community and, soon, we started making plans for Project Nine Mile, a computer education initiative for the students at Stepney.

Che has managed to arrange a couple of computers for the Stepney All Age School in St. Ann. Right now we are in email correspondence about the arrangement. [March 8, 2008, 9:04am, CB]

That was all I heard from Che for a while as he had gone about tying together some loose ends on his side. In the meantime, I was enjoying life again. With some money in my bank account once more, I could return to enjoying nature again. I spent a lot of time at Lesley's home, which was next to a secluded river nestled in the rural hills above Gordon Town, Saint Andrew. There were more trips to the countryside and I made many attempts to link up with Mama G (also known as Gloria Simms) so that she could take me and my friends to unexplored sections of Jamaican land. For some reason, we could never align our schedules though, and I eventually stopped pursuing the possibility. Also, Reggie and I had been regular patrons of Bembe Thursdays (at Weekenz) for well over a year by then. We hardly missed any because we found it to be shining example of what Jamaica's cultural tourism could offer – excellent, raw, dancehall-driven partying that tried to conform to the Noise Abatement Act. My mother and I were on speaking terms again after going through the lowest point in our relationship, and she bought Barack Obama's book, *Dreams from My Father*, for me during a trip abroad. When she returned, a recording of my speech at the Symposium had just begun being aired on the Public Broadcasting Corporation of Jamaica (PBCJ) in regular rotation. I think that she was beginning to comprehend my aspirations around that time. All in all, my personal life was in good shape.

Meanwhile, I was still occupied with IL as we were in a reconstruction phase. Karelle was soon gone from the team and others stepped up to run IL Forumz, notably Annya Campbell-Douglas and Kamala 'Mala' Nicholson (now Johnson). We instituted a new method for communicating with each other and things were beginning to feel efficient again.

As far as Reasoning went, I was still highly critical of our productions, and even harder on myself, but we were experiencing satisfactory growth overall. My attention once again turned to Diageo and the Red Stripe brand when, in a strange attempt to rebound from the "Amistad and friends" debacle, it withdrew its support from hardcore dancehall events in order to make a public statement about the moral state of dancehall. The news frenzied the mainstream media and I was ready to add fuel to the fire. It also got a little personal when I attended Bembe and saw a man take the stage to explain the situation to the crowd (on behalf of Red Stripe it seemed). He was the very promoter who outcompeted me in 2004 when I staged *I-20*. I really wanted to go after the establishment at that point. I decided to call Mr. Maxwell to hear his thoughts about the latest phase of the Red Stripe fiasco. I expected him to support my opinions and give me the confidence to move forward with my plans but he was much more objective about the situation and, by the end of our conversation, I was less inclined to be too confrontational. The next day, April 13, 2008, Ian Boyne, the popular newspaper columnist and television personality, wrote an article called *'Red Stripe hits negative dancehall.'* My relationship with the name, Ian Boyne, was quite unique at the time. In October 2007, I read his column and disagreed with his opinion, writing a response letter to the editor of the Jamaica Gleaner. My letter was published on the same day that a Reasoning episode aired and I hardly hesitated in bragging about my name being in the paper. From that point onward, I continued to portray Mr. Boyne as an unintentional enemy of the youth. Just like I did with Red Stripe, I exploited various opportunities in order to shine a light on Mr. Boyne's views that were disagreeable to me. In February 2008, I responded to another of his articles with yet another letter to the editor. Again, it was published and, all the time, I was throwing words at him on select Wednesday nights. Even though I was learning humility day by day, I was still accompanied by a lot of the arrogance from my teenage years. So it was a pleasure as well as a knock off my high horse when I read Mr. Boyne's latest article:

I feel like today is my day. Ian Boyne has humbled me in his column... In it he managed to make reference to Reasoning while addressing everything I've ever said, in opposition to him, on air. His journalism is superior. [April 13, 2008, 4:04pm, CB]

I remember analyzing myself around that time and realizing that my approach towards Boyne was a form of attention seeking. At the time, I had fantasies in my mind of being able to co-host a television show with him, whereby we could express and debate the general views of two different generations. My taunts were merely my way of trying to engage somebody who I respected. After reading that April piece, I emailed Mr. Boyne so that he could know that I meant no harm or disrespect towards him. I never received a response.

Eventually, I began to focus on the remnants of hatred within me and I wanted all of it to be gone. I wanted to start being a proponent for peace, love and unification rather than separatism and war. The very promoter who contributed to my great financial loss in 2004 was suddenly sitting in the studio with us one Wednesday night. He discussed the views of his major sponsor and we appreciated his presence. I found love in my heart for him thereafter. (Similarly, I would later feel called upon to demonstrate my growing desire for generational unity by interacting with Mullings, who I viewed as another person who wronged me.) Around that time, I also found a wealth of helpful quotations attributed to Rev. Dr. Martin Luther King, Jr., some of which I quote below:

"Man must evolve for all human conflict a method which rejects revenge, aggression and retaliation. The foundation of such a method is love."

"The hope of a secure and livable world lies with disciplined nonconformists who are dedicated to justice, peace and brotherhood."

"The question is not whether we will be extremists, but what kind of extremists we will be... The nation and the world are in dire need of creative extremists."

I wrote those and more in my Career Book on April 29, 2008. By the end of May, Che had sent another Canadian, Mina Mikhail, to Jamaica to spend the next few weeks launching Project Nine Mile.

11
AND THEN THERE WAS HIS IMPERIAL MAJESTY

I had grown to accept the Rastafari faith as a part of my identity, particularly after all the blessings that I had to acknowledge during my tenure at the Museum, and especially following my personal empowerment in February. I was very careful not to declare it out loud though, the reason being that I observed many so-called Rastafarians, like many so-called Christians, living in ways that did not seem compatible with the livity (read: lifestyle) that they touted. Having read Haile Selassie's autobiographical account, *My Life and Ethiopia's Progress*, I desired to emulate the noblest aspects of his personality. I did not want to be counted among the fashion dreads and those who used the popularity of the Rastafari philosophy for public notoriety, so I barely declared to myself, let alone anyone else, that I was a Rasta man. Yet, many recognized Rasta in me, even before I did.

One of my favorite books was *Overstanding Rastafari: Jamaica's Gift to the World* by Yasus Afari and I meditated on it heavily during the months of the spring season. It was a driving force behind my aspirations of universal love. I got a new lease on life and I was counting seemingly endless blessings. It was a truly happy time for me before the ugly head of financial poverty re-emerged. Once again, I had to think about my next steps towards generating income and I was getting depressed at a rapid rate.

At the depth of my emotional rut, I was so tired of applying for jobs and being turned away based on my appearance that I finally said to myself that I would cut my hair. I considered how much easier it would be if I would simply groom myself to the liking of the establishment. My mother was able and more than willing to help me get my foot in the door at the Bank of Nova Scotia, the company for which she worked. I can still remember the night that I was lying in bed, rehearsing my intentions in my mind; I would wake up the next morning, brush my teeth, eat something from the kitchen and walk down the Boulevard to the barbershop. It was the first time that I had fully decided to do it, despite consistently thinking about it ever since the last time I cut my hair, which was shortly before I left Monte Carlo one year prior. There was nothing imaginable that could possibly change my mind the next morning. Then again, one thing that did not cross my mind was the possibility of a very vivid and impactful dream. My jotting the next morning captured more details than I can recount these years later.

I am opening and readjusting my eyes to this realm. I had a very odd dream that I was... somewhere... and it was like a videogame at first. I think I was on a very serious mission. It eventually transitioned to a room where I seemed to have been preparing for something. Then a certain day arrived and not long after midnight I was... beaten? Scorned? Punished?.. I think... for no reason that I was aware of. For the rest of the day I avoided two women, one a mother-like figure, the other her assistant who was like an aunt or something to that effect. As I was hiding in an obscure corner by the door that led outside, under a pile of work clothes apparently there for laundry, I saw that the women were getting ready to leave via a car at the door... half the vehicle inside the room. In the backseat was Haile Selassie I and, just when I noticed, somebody (one of the ladies?) shouted that it is time for me to get in the car and go with them. I had a mistrust of the situation not knowing where they would take me... seeing Ras Tafari gave me the confidence to board the vehicle. As we drove though the countryside, I noticed that Jamaica (where we seemed to be) looked picturesque and stunning –

almost like the quality of the latest digital televisions with high definition – through the windscreen and side windows of the car.

His Imperial Majesty questioned the state of my studies and whether I will be able to stay for another month and a half to finish the course; he seemed disappointed when I said that I would probably not be there for so long. One thing was clear: he needed me, he was counting on me to further his cause. Then, as we were passing a rural field... the horizon wide open with the glow of a setting sun, the King died. First he started getting dizzy, then his brain began to scramble, which I knew because I could now see a little screen (like the free mini black and white televisions that Digicel had given away recently). The images were strange, random and disturbing, changing every second or so. The last image was of a baby that grew a very large penis... Selassie fainted to his death.

He knew he would die.

With little time to spare, he summoned me.

For what? I don't know. [May 13, 2008, 8:10am, CB]

I have been a great interpreter of my own dreams in life but, to this day, I have not fully decoded that dream. The parts that I immediately began to overstand (read: understand) were recorded later that night.

A male baby... a big penis. The poor infant obviously doesn't know how to use or manage the organ. Our young males are in crisis. They (we) are developing in our (their) bodies but not in our (their) minds and souls. In Jamaica... in the United States... in Africa... young black males are decaying. We are laying on the operating table (as the baby in my dream was) waiting to be operated on by Babylon doctors. No wonder Selassie passed out; he must have been unable to withstand the stress, I have no doubt that the King is turning in his grave. I need to direct my efforts to helping young males.

H.I.M. Haile Selassie I is losing his aura as globalization occurs. The Rasta message needs to be updated for the times so that it doesn't lose its potential to affect positive change. I believe that there is a specific role for me to play in this regard. [May 13, 10:43pm, CB]

Months later, I recorded my thoughts on another aspect of the dream, describing Haile Selassie I as the headmaster of the university (represented by the room with the dirty laundry) and still likening the two women in the dream – the female administrators of this university of life – to my mother and one of her sisters, who has historically been the strict disciplinarian of my family.

On June 11, Che presented me with an opportunity to potentially work in Toronto, pending an application process. On June 25 at approximately 5:30pm, he called me to confirm that I had been selected to be on the planning committee for an exciting new initiative that would revitalize the arts and culture industries across the western hemisphere. Upon checking a calendar, I realized that it was about six weeks since my dream and since I had decided to put the barbershop visit on hold; I had waited for precisely a month and a half as instructed by His Imperial Majesty. From first-hand experience I learned the true meaning of the term, "follow your dreams," and I was rewarded with an assigned mission.

But, first, I had to earn it.

12
PREPARING FOR WAR

I was going to be one of five Regional Coordinators for the inaugural *Ignite The Americas* youth arts forum. I was going to be paid a substantial stipend for a comfortable amount of work and I was in a joyous mood again. I was getting ready to go to Canada for the first time in my life and it was an exciting time for me. And then...

I learnt of some unexpected obstacles from Che today. At least, there is one obstacle – the Jamaican government. He called me after midday to update me; apparently, the Canadian government approved me and relayed correspondence to the appropriate ministry here on the Rock as they have with the other countries... While these countries reciprocated approval in a matter of hours, it has been days and Jamaica has not approved me. I highly suspect corruption and fowl play at the moment. The red tape and bureaucracy will be the death of this nation, clearly. [July 9, 2008, 3:02pm, CB]

The appreciation for love and peace that I recently began to cultivate in my heart was probably the major factor stopping me from resorting to acts of aggression against the state. Nevertheless, I was not in the mood for any manifestations of the status quo, a fact that was captured by my journal entry two days later.

Yesterday I went to the Pegasus Hotel with Carrol to attend a Lay Magistrates award dinner. The governor-general and the British high commissioner were in attendance. While I believe that both gentlemen and all the old people in attendance are good people, I found the occasion quite pretentious and annoying...

After such a contamination of my spirit, I immediately changed into some comfortable clothes (although I was very sharp in my suit) and walked to Bembe for a purging. [July 11, 2008, 2:27pm, CB]

A few hours after writing that, I put on a fantastic anniversary party for IL, free of cost in the parking lot of a supermarket on Constant Spring Road. The next day, my world turned upside down:

Understatement of the day: I am angry... A phone call from Che woke me up; Jamaica did not approve me for Ignite The Americas. To add insult to injury, they suggested (appointed?) one of the national youth ambassadors to take my spot and my money. This officially counts as an act of hostility. I pity my country's leaders for their lack of awareness about who they are dealing with... [July 13, 2008, 3:03am, CB]

I started making anxious phone calls, seeking a solution but, if I couldn't get one, I would at least spread the information so far that it would make the papers before the next Reasoning, at which point I would intensify the campaign tenfold. As far as I was concerned, I was getting a lesson in the de facto genocide of the Jamaican youth being committed by their very own government. I did not want to become a member of a party (or a youth party) in order to enjoy the financial benefits of my own will power. Furthermore, Haile Selassie I did not ask me to exercise patience in order to be shafted in this way. There was a plan for me and it involved going to Toronto, that's all I knew. On July 14, I had prepared some letters – I recall one for the Minister of Culture and Youth (and other portfolios that were under her responsibility) and one for the Prime Minister – and went with my mother to her office so as to use her printer. Her co-workers must have been curious about why I was there and Carrol told them about my dilemma. To my absolute surprise, one co-worker knew the Minister of Culture personally, even calling her "Aunty Babsy!"

Suddenly, I found myself on the phone, speaking with Jamaica's minister of information, culture, youth and sports, and she was apparently at her home... she told me to put my issues in writing and meet her at her office. Luckily, I was ahead of her and halfway there. The meeting was short and positive, and I was re-approved for the trip to Toronto. Just like that. [July 14, 2008, 9:24pm, CB]

I remember the sweet feeling of victory that I experienced that day. I thought the battle might have been lost, and I was already looking ahead to the rest of the war, when, in fact, I was victorious from the moment I believed in Haile Selassie I. Without that belief, I would not have made it as far as my mother's downtown office in order to set off that chain reaction. The King did not seem to mind that I prepared for war, but he wanted to direct me to the shortcut of peace. With that in mind, I prepared to meet the culture of Toronto.

13
SWEET MAPLE SYRUP

It surely feels good to be on a mission and to generate an income – a substantial one – in the process. [July 22, 2008, 12:08am, CB]

Those words summarized my general mood and temperament following three days of acquainting myself with Toronto and the *Ignite The Americas* team. I was enchanted by the entire experience and the quality of individuals concentrated in one collective. The core team consisted of Torontonians who were very welcoming and efficient people. I immediately gravitated to Gavin Sheppard, the founder of the Remix Project who arrived at the airport to greet me, as well as countless others. I also met the other four Regional Coordinators: Panmela Castro from Brazil, Jorge Salazar from Canada, Lia Samantha from Colombia and Toki Wright from the USA. We immediately gelled together while maintaining our individualities. We had a series of meetings and gatherings, after which we went our separate ways to begin the work. Back in Jamaica, I was energized and eager to immerse myself in another phase of life. It was as though I was sitting at the table, hungry, awaiting a meal, and I began to detect the scent of revolution being brought to me from heaven's kitchen. Better yet, it was as though I was looking at a stack of pancakes before me, knife and fork at the ready, and then here came the sweet,

sweet maple syrup, no preservatives, no additives. I was about to be satisfied.

With renewed motivation, plus income for the next few weeks, I focused on soliciting potential applicants to represent the Caribbean nations. *Ignite The Americas* was being staged under the auspices of the Organization of American States (OAS), particularly its Inter-American Committee on Culture (CIC), and our aim was to have two delegates represent each OAS member state. Ideally, one male and one female youth artist or advocate would be selected from each country in the western hemisphere – the Americas, which consisted of North America, South America and the West Indies (Caribbean). The unfortunate exception was Cuba, which was not an OAS member state; this became the cause of recurring protests among the more revolutionary minded participants. Soon, we had a fair number of applications to peruse and I made my recommendations to the *Ignite* secretariat. Most of my choices became the official delegates for their countries. I already knew at least two of them, namely Choc'late Allen and Maria Hitchins.

I first came across Choc'late's name in January 2007, when she was featured on local television news for the revolutionary act of fasting for days in a call for the end of crime in her country, Trinidad and Tobago. One year later, she stood before me in the *Africa Unite – Smile Jamaica 2008* office, a bright and charming adolescent girl, just as she had appeared on television. I would experience her infectious and uplifting energy first-hand, particularly at Liberty Hall on that February 6 when she spoke to the audience immediately before I delivered my own speech. Her message of taking personal responsibility resonated with most, if not all who were in attendance. It was widely speculated that she was a returned spirit from ancient times, and that was the first time I genuinely considered reincarnation as a reality on Earth. Just as Che knew that he wanted me to be in Toronto, he and I both knew that she would also have to be there as well. Regardless, just as I had to undergo an application process, so did Choc'late.

Maria was a lady who I met through Reggie, who took the soonest opportunity to include her in the group of regular panelists for Reasoning. I was a big fan of her outspoken, militant personality and thought that she was a great addition to the team. She was also a dance choreographer and I really wanted to have a Jamaican dancer represent the country at *Ignite*, mainly because I thought that Jamaica was already globally known for its music and that it would be a great eye-opener for many people to learn of the latest developments in street dancing. I also tried to arrange for a popular group of street dancers, called Dance Xpressions, to attend the forum as one of the "industry leaders" to speak to the delegation. Unfortunately, that opportunity slipped through the cracks and there was no Jamaican industry leader in Toronto that September. Maria was slightly older than the 30-year-old age limit at the time, but I urged her to apply regardless. She turned out to be the most impressive female applicant from Jamaica and I consulted with the *Ignite* secretariat so that her application would not be disregarded. Upon my recommendation, she was later accepted to be one of the Jamaican delegates. The male delegate was Gregory Simms, a young man who I had not heard of prior to that process. He also had an impressive application and I wanted to see what an individual with his list of accomplishments and responsibilities could contribute to a gathering of such significance and symbolism as *Ignite The Americas*.

On September 11, I was on an Air Jamaica flight to North America. Upon landing in Toronto, I was profiled and sent to join a long line to be interrogated; my official documents from the Canadian government did not seem to matter on this occasion. The immigration officer was a nice and jolly man who insisted that I call him "Sir Snow" and we had a friendly conversation about his many years on the job. He told me that he had met Bob Marley and Peter Tosh much in the same way that he had just met me. I found it uncanny, especially because I had uncannily encountered Mrs. Stewart at the airport in Kingston just before checking in for my flight. In retrospect, given the impact that I had in Canada, I must acknowledge that the spirit of those legendary Wailers must have intentionally been in my presence the whole time.

Once again, the city of Toronto mesmerized me. We had a few days in which to prepare for the arrival of the delegates and I started to make myself at home. The hostel where we slept was located at the corner of Spadina and King streets, a pleasant location. One evening, as Toki and I began to make the half an hour trek from *Ignite* headquarters to the hostel, we got a ride from one of our new Canadian friends, Nana. As we travelled, she unintentionally disobeyed a stop sign and an officer of the law signaled her to stop the vehicle. She, nor her original passenger, Ryan, was aware that I had a half-smoked spliff on my person until I chose to inform them at that moment. Ryan quickly lit a cigarette in an attempt to mask any fragrance emitted by the illegal substance. Behind him was Toki and I sat behind Nana.

The female officer came up... to see her documents and I had cracked my window a bit. Even though Ryan lit a cigarette in our best interest, I still feared the overbearing scent of the herbs. Like a movie scene, the cop leaned in and looked at me... then said, "Put your seatbelt on, hun."
So I did. Then, she was attending to the driver again for all of 5 seconds, if that much, before she did a double-take with an urgency that made me think she surely must have caught a whiff of the high grade.
"By the way... sorry about calling you 'hun.' I got in trouble for calling a lady that yesterday."
That was hilarious in retrospect. What a story to tell... [September 14, 2008, 1:53am, CB]

Throughout the two weeks there, I spent considerable time with my "twin," Gavin Sheppard, and also Mina, who took me to see the Michael Lee-Chin Crystal and to eat at a nice local spot called Hemmingway's. I met Kate Fraser for the first time as she was managing *Ignite's* relationship with the hostel; she would later become involved with Project Nine Mile. A first generation Canadian of Ethiopian parentage, named Addis, also became a fast friend of mine.

By the time the delegates started arriving, I was already very tired. I remember being very annoyed with a delegate from Saint Vincent and the Grenadines on the night that she and her male counterpart arrived. To begin with, I selected neither of them during the application process; in fact, I don't recall either of them applying at all. I only remember that the Vincentian government essentially did what the Jamaican government attempted to do to me by sending two people of its own choosing. This lady in particular was well over 30 years old, and halfway to 40, which was funny to me because of my previous dilemma with Maria, who was just barely older than the age limit at the time. The more upsetting part was that, on the day of her arrival, this lady was issuing complaints, introducing an energy that was misaligned with the spirit of the gathering, and, as a result, causing a number of persons to approach me to address her behavior. I was clearly out of patience as I called the government of Saint Vincent "retarded and narrow-minded" in my journal entry on September 15. After a night's rest, I found my interactions with her much more pleasant. I recall that she offered apologies for her prior behavior and explained that she did not travel in ideal fashion the day before. She was also feeling a little ill and I gave her my attention, even getting some tea for her to drink. By the end of the forum, she was a very enjoyable character to be around, even though I analyzed that she was unmistakably there to promote her government, whether or not she was conscious of doing so.

The forum itself was five days of discussions, during which all these young, passionate people discussed the nature of the creative industries in their respective nations and offered suggestions for further development. We also divided ourselves into three teams to strategize on: firstly, creating a hemispheric-wide network of youth artists; secondly, developing toolkits that could effectively be distributed through said network to the remotest parts of the Americas; and thirdly, influencing the culture policies of the OAS member governments in order to facilitate the responsible growth of the creative industries as driven by the youth. I was a part of the first group. As usual, the Career Book documented my thoughts and emotions.

The first day of the forum went well. For me, coming off of my caffeine rush, it was a drag, and the speech did not turn out as I envisioned it. Regardless, I was very happy with my work group; we are responsible for building the hemispheric network...

The Governor-General of Canada, a charming lady of Haitian ancestry, visited us as well. I would have seen her a second time if I hadn't knocked out when we were supposed to go to Casa Loma for a formal function. [September 17, 2008, 1:56am, CB]

Yesterday was a little more than good for me. We went to the Center for Spanish-Speaking Peoples on Jane Street. Kris, the facilitator assigned to my group, told me that the area was designated a "priority neighbourhood" – it's a term that typically describes communities with a high immigrant culture. This area definitely had a strong Jamaican presence. I heard at least one well-pronounced "claat" and got some nice stew chicken at Willy's Jerk.

At the meeting we learned how to break dance... and we also did some drumming with a talented young Latino who could be stereotyped easily as a gangbanger in the USA. The discussions about our objectives were stimulating and focused...

After a nap, Kate, Toki and I got a ride with Addis to go to a hiphop performance but it ended before we got there at about 11:30pm/midnight. We went to a bar close to the hostel instead; this was after I spoke on Reasoning over the phone in an alley way...

Before my early evening nap, I had enlightening conversations... We talked about Cuba and, also, the CIC's general differences with the rest of the OAS. Meanwhile, at the end of the night... some of us were discussing how to effectively change our Saturday meeting to a closed door session – no facilitators, no cameras. [September 18, 2008, 7:34am, CB]

After that entry, I did not write for about six days. I was very involved and constantly occupied. Until then, I had been stealing a few minutes before going to sleep or right after waking up in the mornings to update my journal but I soon learned to treasure even those few minutes as moments for rest and meditation. On

September 24, I finally wrote a long entry summarizing the milestones of those days that I did not thoroughly document. Mostly, it was about my experiences at Manifesto events and further explorations of the city. One particular incident was so important to me, and presumably the *Ignite The Americas* cause, that I later recounted it in detail after my return to Jamaica. The event was the final meeting on the forum agenda. After spending those few days developing our proposal for youth-led contributions to the development of the creative industries, we aligned our final day, September 19, to coincide with an annual CIC meeting of OAS culture representatives so that we could present our case to them and solicit their feedback. My words on September 29 vividly described the setting:

After we, the youth, made our presentation to the 14 OAS officials (of 34 invited nations), some of whom had no clue about the conscience of culture departments of their own nations, we opened the floor to responses from said officials. Celia Toppin from Barbados and the high-ranking culture ministry official from Brazil both contributed satisfactorily to the discussion. The St. Vincent representative did not contribute anything; in fact, he disappeared from the table after a time. Not surprising... one of the delegates sent by that government to replace our choice, decided to waste our time with a PR statement about the greatness of her government. Very irritating.

The USA official expressed sympathy and care regarding our cause, and even went as far as to let us know of her background in the arts. Unfortunately, she smoked me out of my hole when she said that "money doesn't come overnight," so we need to think of more non-monetary requests.
[September 29, 2008, 6:48pm, CB]

At that moment, I immediately indicated to the moderator that I was interested in adding my opinion to the discussion, and I sat there and waited for my turn, noticing that nobody else had responded to the brazen statement that irked me so easily. When I was finally asked to speak, I remember being on the verge of unleashing an angry tirade that would have introduced a new level of negativity to the room. Just before opening my mouth though, I suddenly realized that I had nothing against this woman from the USA. My issue was with the hypocrisy that I perceived as coming from United States policy and it became clear to me that the lady had the unfortunate job of representing a government that paid her to say certain things. Nevertheless, I thought that she had to be punished for saying those words, just as a baby could be punished by its loving parents in order to be taught the difference between right and wrong. When I spoke in that instant, I expressed my appreciation for her approach. I told the delegation that I sensed that she was a good person. After making that clear, I then said that I found it hard to believe that the USA, of all nations, could tell the youth that money didn't come overnight when money was found overnight to go to war. I thought that the USA was exposing itself as a purveyor of death, so much so that it would remorselessly reject the notion of supplying funds to facilitate a movement of youth in the arts, an industry largely characterized by peaceful expressions of the self. I expressed as much into the microphone before venturing to touch on another unrelated point that I wanted to address during my long wait for undivided attention. After about a sentence though that second part, the Spanish and Portuguese translators seemed to have just finished translating my first point for the benefit of my South American counterparts and the room consequently erupted into a loud applause. It was at that moment that my popularity skyrocketed; that night and thereafter I felt like I was being treated like a hero. It was like I had addressed the United Nations and I had channeled a combination of the spirits of Che Guevara and Haile Selassie I.

Upon my return home, I felt like I had a crucial role to play in ensuring that what was started in Toronto would quickly take root in Jamaica.

I came to the realization... that I brought my FIREMACHINE* with me to Toronto for an event called Ignite The Americas. The irony increases when

---

* The FIREMACHINE was my Toshiba laptop, which I bought in 2007 and named almost immediately, because I intended for it to be an important tool in my bid to spark an unforgettable flame. On the morning of Taiwo's funeral, I was showering to go, with the FIREMACHINE playing music next to the shower as usual, when it

I think about the fact that my Toshiba was in the minority amidst a lot of Apple Macbooks. This situation summarizes my self-perceived role in this movement. I don't exactly consider myself a true artist but I love to surround myself with the arts. Mac users are generally artistic people; these are the people I believe in and want to defend. My fire is here to blaze a path for them to charge forward... and I will sacrifice myself more than willingly to make them advance as much as possible. [September 29, 2008, 1:30am, CB]

---

accidentally and freakishly fell into the shower with me and was completely soaked by water and shampoo, which added to my feeling of sadness that day. Miraculously, it was rehabilitated and continued to operate (barely at times) until my important task was done. By the time described at the end of this book, the FIREMACHINE finally started showing signs of completely giving out but I continue to appreciate its service to the revolution. It fulfilled its purpose as its name suggests.

14
THE DRAGON

Following the interpretation of my dream in May, I reflected and meditated seriously on what I thought was my implied mission. I came to a number of conclusions within myself. I would set an example for the youth, particularly young males; that was the first thing. Second, I would deliberately attempt to play a role in the spiritual development of humanity. I wondered if, through the dream, the Universe was urging me to take responsibility for ushering in a new way of thinking that transcended the popularity of religious doctrines and other philosophies, including the Rastafari livity. I honestly felt like Selassie I himself had reassured me that he was going to help me to adapt his own message to the present time. Obviously, that was not something that I wanted to say out loud but I felt it in the most sincere and non-egotistical way possible. Thinking about the process of self-discovery that began when I lost that CSA presidential election and continued with Taiwo's passing and, again, with my experience at the *Africa Unite Youth Symposium*, I can safely say that it was that dream in the spring of 2008 that catapulted my thinking to the level of finally accepting that I had to embrace my individuality and strengthen myself in order to strengthen the human collective that I concerned myself with so much. Before the end of that summer, I shut down IdlerzLounge.com. The opportunity came when it was hacked but the truth was that I was very frustrated with myself for serving others at the expense of my own well-being, and also that the vast majority of those who I served seemed not to appreciate my sacrifices. I didn't want to further resent what was once my most beloved pet project, so, after its 8th anniversary party in the supermarket parking lot, I decide that I would not make any more attempts to put it back online. It was one of the hardest decisions I ever made. I was probably more attached to that website than its many addicted members combined.

Around that time, I decided to register a domain name called Duttyism.com. The intention was that I would focus on myself for the first time in years and I would do it in plain view of the public. After my obligations with *Ignite The Americas* were done, I was going to start planning the launch of that site, or so I said to myself, but there were other plans for me.

I had a strong urge to relocate to Florida and it was the kind of inner feeling that I never dared to resist. In fact, a similar feeling overcame me as I completed my university studies. I knew that there was no way that I was going to stay in Florida or anywhere else on the North American continent after school. I had a sense of prewritten destiny awaiting me in Jamaica and that sixth sense fueled my decision to book the flight. Many people did not realize that I was in possession of a "green card," which meant that I had permanent residency status in the United States. Many of those who knew could not comprehend my decision to leave, or, otherwise, they were in disagreement with the decision. Countless people wanted that legal way out of Jamaica and into the USA, yet there I was, a young man with a green card that he was not enthusiastic about having. That piece of plastic, of course, has continuously proven to be a great asset along my journey as in this case when I was led by my intuition to return and attempt to set up a comfort zone in the country that I had fled two years earlier. I made preparations to go to Fort Lauderdale after completing my *Ignite The Americas* duties.

I travelled to my new base in Miramar, Florida on October 16, 2008. Before departing from Jamaica, I wrote what was intended to be my final entry in the Career Book. It started as follows:

This is the day I leave Jamaica. Today I will step into a foggy future yet trod sure-footed with inner clarity... [October 16, 2008, 2:34am, CB]

At the time, I had a deep paranoia about the possibility of my personal belongings being confiscated and inspected by officials at United States airports. I decided not to bring my Black Book or Career Book with me on the journey. It was a hard decision for me because I was generally never without them, unless I travelled for a weekend or some other short period of time. This time though, I was certain that I did not want those books to be anywhere within the geographic confines of Babylon's most efficient national system. I much preferred to leave them in Jamaica so that they could benefit other revolutionary youth there if anything unfortunate was to happen to me while I investigated the reason for my newfound calling.

Upon landing in Fort Lauderdale, the first thing on my agenda was to acquire a new journal. I visited my favorite bookstore at the time, figuring that I would probably not find one to my liking. I was very picky about the appearance of my journals. The Black Book was given to me during my time at ERAU; it was a birthday gift from a friend. I loved it very much because it was plain and void of the word "journal" on the cover, which was a feature that always irked me about journals sold in stores. I was extremely private and I thought that journals were supposed to be equally discreet by their very nature and purpose. When the Black Book was exhausted, it took me about a month to find another useful book in which I could continue my jottings. During the hiatus, I had no interest in writing a word unless I found the right book. Unfortunately, the selection among all of Kingston's popular bookstores and pharmacies was not quite as broad in range as a single, typical Barnes & Noble location. I had to settle for a large, green book on which the following words were printed on the front in golden font:

CAREER
INDEX
QUIRE BOOK
3Q

I simply referred to it as my Career Book. On the inside, there were tabbed pages with twenty-six distinct sections for the letters of the English alphabet. The abnormalities were the two 'M' sections and the single section for both 'X' and 'Z,' which were at the end after the 'Y' section. It so happened that, on October 16, 2008, my entry finished the last page in the 'T' section. When I realized that, I could not help but acknowledge the unknown that awaited me in the USA. Later on, because of my life-altering experience in Florida, I decided to continue writing in the Career Book. In doing so, I deliberately skipped the 'U' section in honor of the contents of my third named journal, which I would like to say that I found but it was more like it found me.

There I was in the bookstore, seeking my new set of paper sheets bound in hard cover. I walked directly to the area with the selection of journals, prepared to dislike the majority and equally prepared to sit down with two or three of them for a few minutes in order to make a decision. To my delight, I immediately saw it as soon as I bent the corner. It was a most attractive blend of olive and black. It was smaller than I was used to but not too small to cause discomfort; in fact, it was slightly larger than one of Moleskine's large notebooks, which I was introduced to earlier in the year by Mina and loved very much. Best of all, it had no words on it but, in the place of text, on the front cover there was the fascinating symbol of a dragon in golden silhouette. It immediately spoke to me and I was practically unable to resist it. To add to the allure, it was the last one of its kind remaining on the shelf, as I could only assume that others like it were in the store before my arrival. I felt like this book with the dragon on it was indelibly connected to whatever force was responsible for making me go to Florida. I quickly scanned the rest of the available journals, mostly out of respect for my usual process, and then made my way to the cashier. By the time I had started writing in it, it already had its name: the Dragon Book. What I was supposed to write in there was a later concern of mine but I already began to feel like I was about to undergo a unique and important ritual of initiation and I was very happy to have found the Dragon Book so that I could begin to record my thoughts and experiences along the way.

The reality was that I had lots to document while I lived in Florida. In about two weeks, I found that I had come face to face with the most unexpected of forces. When I analyzed it and its relentless pursuit of my sanity, I could think of no other way to refer to it than "the dragon." It was pervasive and tireless, and had me under constant surveillance. By the time December arrived, I was happy to have the opportunity to go back to Jamaica but I knew I did not yet accomplish a victory. After a few days of relative inner peace, I went directly back to Florida to finish my mission. By then, I knew very well what I was supposed to do and I wanted to document everything for the benefit of future generations, even if only for my own offspring. It took me about three more weeks, under intense mental stress, to gather and document a satisfactory amount of data and evidence for the purpose at hand. Another week elapsed before I was able to get myself and the Dragon Book safely back to Jamaica. I have no intention of revealing the contents of that book until I feel satisfied with my post-analysis but it is something that I think will be of value to somebody on Earth at the appropriate hour.

During the three or so months that I danced with the dragon, I also did a bit of cross-country travelling. I visited the city of Chicago for the first time, where I stayed with Klipp, and took some time to investigate the neighborhood of Altgeld Gardens, where presidential candidate Barack Obama was known to build his political capital through dealing with an asbestos situation. Days later, on November 4 (my 26th birthday), Mr. Obama was elected to the office of the president of the USA. Later that month, I visited Clint in New York, where I discovered Strand's bookstore and purchased some impactful books. Finally, I went to Washington, DC to witness the historic inauguration of President Obama. I had hoped to see more of the world but, following the completion of my crash course in the nature of the dragon, I went back to Jamaica where my path continued.

2009

15
A REVOLUTIONARY NAME

On January 27, 2009, only days before my departure from Florida, I visited a good friend of mine, Tasha, who lived a reasonable distance away from my base. On my previous visit, she introduced me to a cozy coffee shop that was quite to my liking. It so happened that we met there again on the second occasion, along with other friends of hers. By chance, I decided to scan through a special edition of a popular magazine – *Time* or *Life* (I am more inclined to say the latter) – and I discovered the most gratifying information on one of its pages. The word "Dutty" immediately caught my gaze and piqued my interest. I was surprised to have come across that word in such a prestigious-looking magazine, since it was found only in the dialect of Jamaican patois as far as I knew. In one sense, it was a crude way of saying "dirty" but, in another sense, it was a way to describe somebody whose personality mixed a certain arrogance and nonchalance with a disregard for potential consequences. I think it was that quality in me that earned me one of my nicknames, "Dutty," during high school, although I can never remember who first called me by that name. The more I reflect on it, the more I wonder if I might have been the one to declare it first; that was certainly something that I would do at the time. Either way, I embraced the name and I was quite proud of it for many years, so much so that it evolved over time. I was Dutty X, Dutty Man, Dutty Dread and Ras Dutty depending on time or place or person asked. So, in January 2009, having been called "Dutty" for at least a decade, I was beyond myself when I read the magazine article that educated me about a man called Dutty Boukman (interchangeable with Boukman Dutty) who, in Haiti, sparked the only successful slave rebellion in modern history. It must have been that very night, upon returning to my base, that I started to research Dutty Boukman. There was not much information about him but I learned that he originally lived in Jamaica, where the spelling of his name was B-O-O-K-M-A-N, due to the fact that he was a literate slave and he was known to always carry a book with him. He was later sold to a plantation in French-speaking Haiti, where the spelling of his name was changed to B-O-U-K-M-A-N. I felt so empowered by the newfound knowledge that I decided on that day to make a new and probably final adjustment to my beloved nickname. I would promote myself as Dutty Bookman, using the Jamaican version of the name because I was born into the Jamaican version of neo-colonialism. For every aspect of Boukman's life that I knew of, I observed a clear parallel in my own life. I was an avid reader, constantly carried books and writing materials on my person and was most interested in revolutionary activity, although not through violent means. I figured that I possessed the same spiritual temperament as the 18th century icon but my purpose was to implement a 21st century strategy, much in the same way that the film trilogy, *The Matrix*, implied to me that Earthly existence is a cycle and that certain characters must always be present within the system in order to fulfill a pre-determined role in the grand scheme of things. My mission was to expedite a process meant to correct the flaws of the system, causing it to positively update itself, which is how I viewed the role of Boukman's life, culminating in his call to action in 1791. If he determined that bloodshed was necessary in his time, then so it was.

Considering the dangerous situation that I was put through during those Florida days, I felt like the Universe rewarded me for emerging victorious by connecting me to the knowledge of my own predecessor. In the scheme of things, it seemed like I was brought to Florida for the purpose of a training exercise, and having passed the course and grasped the lesson, I was granted more knowledge about my life's purpose. It was a window through which I looked out at my potential future and I had to decide if I was going to fulfill that destiny or not.

16
UNREASONABLE DRAMA

During those months that I spent in Florida, Reggie held down the Reasoning fort with assistance from the core group of panelists. By then, I was already feeling like I did not want the obligation of being at a given place at a given time each week, as much as I loved what we created. In addition to that, I was considering a new vision for the program, where we would not only have a pool of panelists but a pool of potential hosts. A person with a knack for a certain topic deserved to direct the flow of the discussion for any episodes based on that subject matter. I thought of it as "open source" talk radio and I was getting ready to stress the idea to Reggie (if I didn't start already) as a strategy to begin testing in 2009. Surely, my ego loved the growing power associated with being a known constant on the program, and I was a big fan of Jon Stewart and Stephen Colbert; *The Daily Show* and *The Colbert Report* combined to form my favorite hour of television programming. Regardless, had I been given the opportunity to spread the power around to other worthy personalities, I am certain that it would have been done. It was just a matter of proper timing. Sadly, a series of unfortunate events prevented any chance of realizing that vision in the near future.

The first disaster was the installment of a certain Miss Harrison as the new general manager of NewsTalk 93FM. It happened while I was away and Reggie was wary as he described her to me. She seemed to have been on a mission to re-organize the station in the swiftest and most relentless fashion. People were visibly upset with her from the moment she arrived. Some people were fired and producers were being dictated some take-it-or-leave-it terms for changing the format of their programs. By the time of my brief intermission from dueling with the dragon, Harrison had requested to meet with us to discuss the direction of our talk show. After that meeting, I was equally as wary as Reggie and, as was usually my style, tried very hard to give her the benefit of any doubt out of respect for the spirit of love that I was still working to embody.

The NewsTalk lady was a talkative, friendly, pretentious person. I appreciate her approach to her work though. She helped us to focus our thoughts on Reasoning. [January 11, 2009, 12:57pm, CB]

In reality, she was trying to encourage us to dilute the potency of our product. She expressed to us, in no uncertain terms, that a NewsTalk under her management would compete with the popular music-driven stations. That was why she hired popular personality, Denise Hunt, to host a new daytime program. Reasoning, as far as she was concerned, had to step up to her level of marketing or face elimination in due time. We humored her and started to brainstorm ways in which we could appease her while maintaining our standard. The real purpose of the meeting though was for her to issue a warning of the inevitable: she was going to sack Reasoning. I subtly told her to beware when I informed her that Reggie was an engineer and I studied rocket science; we were precise, critical thinkers. Most of all, we were radio revolutionaries beyond her understanding. Leaving it on that note, I returned to Florida for the conclusion of my bout with the dragon.

My February return to Jamaica coincided with the arrival of five Canadians – Che, Mina and Kate, as well as Mark Valino, who I met in Toronto, and Tiffany Hsiung, who I was about to meet for the first time. The mission was the continuation of Project Nine Mile and we set out early in the morning on February 6 to go to the Saint Ann community. Since it was about eight months since Mina went there to deliver two laptop computers to Stepney, and train relevant personnel and some children to use them, this trip was a follow-up to evaluate the effect of the gifts at the school. It was also an opportunity for the Canadians to film aspects of community life for a documentary. We had a lot of fun while we stayed there, and the host family treated us very well. After five days or so, we returned to Kingston where I, once again, started to investigate the job market. It was very clear, by then, that a painfully vast majority of establishments were not interested in hiring anybody with "unkempt hair" and I was already on the verge of ceasing to pay my hard-earned money to have my hair maintained for the sake of fashion. I decided to go back to the Museum and ask Mrs. Stewart about any vacancies. She told me that she was in need of a new tour guide and I agreed to be interviewed for the position. I soon began training and, during the first week that I resumed working at 56 Hope Road, I already found inspiration.

I must continue to believe in signs, even if I misread some and imagine others... How can it also be that I find myself working at the Bob Marley Museum again, since Monday, to come to the realization that Marley's last album was 'Confrontation,' which has an album cover depicting Bob on a white horse, piercing a large dragon with his lance. Bear in mind, I have also stabbed the dragon, figuratively, and also bear in mind that the first song that Reasoning played was 'Confrontation' by Damian Marley. [February 26, 2009, 9:58pm, CB]

Around that time, there were rumors at NewsTalk that Miss Harrison's crosshairs were aimed directly at Reasoning. We were about to become the next casualty to add to her tally, which also included engineers and other personnel who devoted years to the station. In the meantime, she was hiring new people, including at least one friend of hers who defected from another station to help her bully and annoy the meek. The more we analyzed the situation, the more we thought that the wisest action was to remove our program from the station ourselves. In a few short weeks, on March 18, 2009 to be specific, we aired a final episode and never returned to NewsTalk. On March 31, 2009, we signed a contract with another station, Bess 100FM, to have a weekly, 4-hour timeslot on Tuesday nights. We were slated to begin in exactly two weeks after that.

Days later, Reggie visited the presumable home of NewsTalk's Mr. Abrahams at his own invitation. I was busy at the Museum at the time and was unable to go. Following the meeting, Reggie gave me his synopsis, which implied that Mr. Abrahams was asking us to return to his station. Reggie informed him that we already signed a contract at Bess 100FM at which point it seemed like Abrahams' posture and demeanor was much more relaxed. He had apparently heard what he needed to hear. We wondered what he had up his sleeve.

Soon, the day that I was eagerly awaiting had arrived. It was April 14 and, hours in advance of our 10:00pm start time, we went to the Bess FM station on East Bloomsbury Road, off of Hagley Park Road in Kingston. When we got there, we had a rude awakening. Without realizing it, we became main characters in a tragic play that involved a popular disc jockey, Gabre Selassie, whose show we greatly respected, as well as station manager, Yvonne Chang, who signed the contract with us, Lou Gooden, a veteran announcer, and Tony Shaw, who I believe owned the station. At the end of a very long and taxing evening, we only gathered that Bess management neglected to inform Gabre that they were removing him from his Tuesday night timeslot in order to facilitate us. In essence, they had two legally binding contracts and had to bully their way out of one – clearly, the new program, Reasoning. It was a very embarrassing incident for me, as we had done a fair amount of promotion to spread the word to Reasoning's fan base that the show was returning to the airwaves. We engaged in many days of public education about Bess 100FM – free advertising for the station since the majority of our loyal audience had never heard of the station prior to our announcement. I was in disbelief that all that was done just for us to be told that we were not going on air on the day and time stipulated in our contract. By then, my Career Book was finished and I was documenting my experiences in a more cryptic way with the use of multiple Moleskine books. I could only summarize the event as *"the most confusion I have ever experienced firsthand."*

After my initial panic, and Reggie's usual, more composed demeanor, we decided to drop the issue for the time being and sought legal advice. The following weekend, Miss Chang proposed to us that we start on the 22nd with a new timeslot: three hours from 2am to 5am. That was certainly insulting, not just to us as individuals or to our program, but also to the youth in general. It was disgusting to me because, in essence, what the new proposal signaled was that the generation represented by Miss Chang was unapologetic about relegating constructive, youth-led initiatives on a whim. It was particularly depressing to me because Bess 100FM was implicitly or explicitly promoting the Rastafari lifestyle – in fact, during our negotiations, Mr. Shaw spent considerable time letting me know that he was a Twelve Tribes man even though he had decided to cut his hair – yet, they were content to dishonor a contract with a conscious, downright revolutionary program and then attempt to have it air when most of the nation's citizens were engaged in the deepest phases of their slumber. A fitting reflection of the intergenerational relationship, I thought.

At our next meeting with Miss Chang, we informed her that we were not going to accept the new timeslot and that was the end of that saga. We preferred to remain off the airwaves before getting involved with the level of disorganization and dishonesty that we observed at Bess 100FM. Meanwhile, there was a rumor that Abrahams was somehow planning to acquire another station, Hot 102FM. I noted the rumor without much significance attached but it would make more sense to me later in the year.

Life went on.

17
SPOT CHECK

The absence of Reasoning disturbed me for a while but I never stopped believing in the conspiracy of the Universe to bring about the conditions needed to dismantle the injustices on the planet. I also never stopped believing that I was an instrument within that conspiracy. In times of despair, anger or other negative human emotions, I always tried to maintain as much faith, pureness of heart and good will as I was capable of. The result has historically been the reception of blessings so great that the memories of the undesirable instances actually bring me joy, in a sense. Plus, with the weekly Reasoning routine suddenly extracted from my existence, I could place more focus on new beginnings that were already underway. There were two very exciting developments taking place and the first was the emerging professional career of a friend of mine who was named Oje Ollivierre at birth, but is more commonly known today as Protoje.

In speaking about my relationship with Oje, I am compelled to begin by describing my relationship with a mutual friend of ours. His name is Kwame 'Stagga' Falconer, a past student of Munro College. We met in 2001 when he enrolled at ERAU and I was beginning my second year there. We shared a love for football and were generally the main attackers on the CSA football team. He was physically big, which deceived opponents since he accelerate quicker than just about anybody who defended against him. He was very aggressive on the field and took very accurate shots at goal. I was a lot smaller, employed more fanciness and flair in my strategy, and was also quick; I often served as a decoy in our runs at goal. I also knew how to get the ball in the back of the net and, one season, I challenged Stagga to determine who would score the most goals. At the end of the season, Stagga had 16 goals, only two more than my 14, but, despite the friendly competition, we never played selfishly in relation to each other. In 2003, we decided to share an off-campus apartment and, through that experience, I really learned a lot about brotherhood and genuine, fraternal love. It was also Stagga who was responsible for letting me listen to the music of his friend, Protoje, for the first time.

Over time, I became a huge fan of Oje's music. I even had a morning ritual that involved playing, on repeat, a certain collaboration with him and Evaflow, another friend of theirs. From then on, I always had a thought in my mind that Protoje was destined to instigate a fresh approach to Jamaican music; and I thought that Evaflow was a different being who would continue to usher that evolution of the art form. Oje and another friend, Currie, visited Stagga at our apartment in Daytona Beach on one or two occasions and that was how I initially became acquainted with him in person. I remember that those early conversations with him caused me to laugh until I experienced pain.

We linked up once every few months at a time and reasoned with each other briefly. On a particular occasion in the middle of my stint at Monte Carlo, I went to Florida when, I guess, I had some consecutive off-days on the weekly schedule (I had to make periodic appearances in the USA to maintain my green card status). Stagga, Capo and I went to link Proto, who was based there at the time, and he treated us, as always, to some singing.

...Proto unleashed some of his new material for my and Capo's virgin ears. Stagga was, of course, already familiar with the songs. I was impressed; Proto continues to grow himself and his craft... The evolution of the global Jamaican consciousness is at hand. [May 22, 2007, 5:13pm, BB]

Those words were written as I reminisced about the song that most impressed me. It had a different working title then, but it would eventually become the 8th track on his debut album (four calendar years later), a song called 'J.A.'

On another occasion, this time in Kingston, we were at a gathering and he was going on the road to get something that we determined necessary for the enhancement of the meditation. I went along with him and, in the car, our mutual respect for each other became apparent. I sensed the potential for cooperation but I had yet no preconceived notions about how our relationship would manifest itself. Not until I dreamed about Haile Selassie I did it begin to dawn on me that Oje and I potentially had the combined capacity to effect significant and positive change in society through our different modes of self-expression. I still did not know what we would create together or how we would do it, but I felt very sure that we had to cooperate on a mission. Then, in January 2009, while I was briefly in Jamaica in the middle of my dance with the dragon, we laid out a blueprint for the year. He was ready to show his face in the mainstream and he planned to release his first official single with an accompanying video before the summer season. He also determined that, in December, he would stage a live show to display the range of his music. Those were the major checkpoints in addition to a few others in between. I told him that I was ready to help. Then I went back to Florida to finish my business with the dragon.

Back in Jamaica again, while I was experiencing the changes in my life as mentioned before, something spectacular happened in a fleeting moment. It was April 10, 2009 – Good Friday or Bad Friday depending on who you asked – indeed a bittersweet night for me. We were driving from a studio in the Windward Road area where the Uprising Roots Band was based. The video for 'Arguments' was already recorded and was going through its post-production process and, the week before, we were introduced to Winston McAnuff, a living legend and father of Uprising Roots drummer, Black Kush. The studio itself was a haven for both of us; for Oje it was a step in the right musical direction, for me it was a great source of spiritual inspiration. On that particular Friday, I was happy to use my new chalice for the first time. All its parts were carefully made and delivered to me by two elder Rasta brethrens whose friendships meant a lot to me – Chicken (who later passed away) and Paul, both of whom I met at the Museum. I waited for the right moment to use the chalice and, finally, had a strong urge to bring it and share its inaugural use with those good souls by Windward Road. After a great evening, Oje and I left the scene and turned northward onto Mountain View Avenue. Perhaps a minute or so later, we encountered a routine spot check and were pulled over directly across the road from the Mountain View police station. By then, I had assured Oje that I had flung my spliff tail out the window, inconveniently forgetting that I did not utilize all of the separate stash reserved for the chalice. I also did not think that the possession of a chalice was an offense unless one also possessed herbs. So, I was quite relaxed.

There were some squadies (regular, low-ranking officers) and one inspector on the scene. The inspector personally dealt with me, the passenger, and took a great interest in my black bag with Bob Marley's face on it in red, yellow and green, surrounded by marijuana leaf symbols. He looked in the bag and was happy to find my chalice and herbs; and he also frisked me so aggressively that I thought he was going to rip my most treasured military jacket. He asked me a barrage of questions and I defiantly fired back responses. Then he ordered the squadies to book me and lock me up. I immediately cooperated and started walking towards the station across the street while Oje ventured to reason with the inspector on my behalf. Having no luck there, he parked the car and went inside the station to join me.

The rest of the night was a big joke to me. I was laughing and making sarcastic comments in earshot of the officers while Oje asked me to calm down. Then, I decided to take out one of my Moleskine books and take notes about my surroundings. Among other things, I wrote down the badge numbers of the three officers in the room. There was '12771,' a red seamed officer who was clearly the apprentice of the group and there was '9490,' who was dressed in gear for urban warfare and who engaged me in a delightful conversation of a psychological nature; in fact, before I located his number, I labeled him as "no number psychologist" in my book. My favorite one though, was '11747,' who did nothing special but he was the one who held the pen that was inking my destiny in a large quire book that reminded me of my Career Book. Periodically, he was the one who had to address me with a question or a statement that he was required to say to me by law or whatever else. Therefore, he was the one who got the brunt of my sarcasm. Regardless, he was very polite to me and I thought that there should be more like him in the police force. The officers came to the conclusion that Oje and I were comedians at heart and we told them that they would be seeing us on their television sets in due time, telling them with the same certainty that we would tell a person the time after looking at our wristwatches. I was informed about my court date, Oje signed as my surety and we were getting ready to leave when the inspector strolled in with all his arrogance – I didn't like him very much. He walked over to me as I was finishing my contributions to the quire book, stood uncomfortably close to me and nonchalantly asked me if I wanted back my weed. I glanced at him, looked back down into the book and returned his nonchalance in telling him that I wanted back my chalice. Behind his back, the 'prentice and '11747' signaled to me in a way that implied they were on my side and wanted me to calm down and just be happy to be able to go home that night. I thought I noticed '9490' holding back an urge to laugh at my retort. Sensing annoyance emerging in the inspector's demeanor, I was happy to hear Oje chime in with blessings and salutations for the law enforcers. We then went directly to the car and drove homeward.

I never quite got over the loss of my chalice. I would have endured any jail time to have it returned to me. I was very upset that I only used it once and my mind soon constructed visions of that police station engulfed in flames. About a week and a half later, I showed up at the Half Way Tree Resident Magistrate's Court for my appointment. That was a whole other ordeal that amused me tremendously. The judge, Judith Pusey, took it upon herself to tell me a story, from which I gathered the implication that I was a "hooligan." I was put behind bars twice for a total time of less than an hour and I paid JM$2,100 to the government for having some vegetation and a chalice made of calabash and a plastic hose. Afterwards, I went directly to a location that Reggie introduced me to and, there, I lit up a spliff and began to meditate on how I was going to get my revenge on the state as represented by the faces of people like the inspector in his khaki uniform and the judge, Judy, who apparently desired her own timeslot on cable television. Reggie soon arrived and we discussed the woes of living in Babylon, then I made my way home. Later that evening, Oje linked me and I sat in his car to hold another meditation. I further vented my frustrations in his presence, and he played a CD with some instrumentals and began to sing one of his new creations for me to critique. Before the meeting was over, I told him that I was going to write a story about the day's events and send to him. He promised to read it and compose a song if he felt inspired.

When I started to write the story, I realized that I had two major acts. The first was the spot check scenario; the second was the courthouse scenario. Then, I further realized that I could divide the day at the courthouse into two lessons. The first was to highlight the arrogance of the actors in the so-called justice system of Jamaica; the second was to describe the scene inside the jail cell and the psychological effects on young people, some of who, like me, were incarcerated for silly reasons. I had three climatic moments to exploit and I decided to make three separate short stories. Then, I started to reflect on the main antagonists – there was the inspector and there was the judge. That was when my most important moment of inspiration arrived. I thought to myself that the people themselves did not bother me as much as the spirit of oppression that they represented. Maybe they even thought that they were humanity's heroes for perpetuating and trying to strengthen the status quo. A feeling of pity for them overcame me. My quarrel was with something more powerful than them, something that they involuntarily obeyed when they woke up in the mornings, something that performed its deeds through the actions of these people. I had the opportunity to observe it at close range only months prior. It was the dragon, the blasted dragon!

Putting the story together was the simplest part of the process. It was fact-based and I now completely overstood its relevance in the context of my own life as well as in the context of revolutionary progress in Jamaica. The words poured out of me, then I looked it over and made the usual minor edits required after my first drafts. On Thursday, April 23, I sent an email to Oje with three attached files; the subject of the email was 'Ammo.'

A short while later, Oje sang a version of 'Wrong Side Of The Law' that brought me absolute delight. From that day forth, I stopped fantasizing about the police station being on fire and grew into a new appreciation for the power of the arts based on personal experience. I had successfully channeled my destructive energy into constructive self-expression and felt an enormous satisfaction from doing so. Out of the dark cloud, instigated by a routine encounter with the Jamaica Constabulary Force, emerged Dutty Bookman and Protoje with a joint purpose.

18
THE DUTTY TUFF

As previously mentioned, there were two exciting developments happening in my life shortly after my return to Jamaica. I expounded on the initial stages of my relationship with Protoje, which was one of them. The second development was related to my formal job in the system. After successfully being trained as a tour guide at the Museum, the most splendid opportunity presented itself to me. There was a relatively urgent need for somebody to go to Tuff Gong International, the record company founded by Bob Marley, Peter Tosh and Bunny Wailer (now owned by Marley's family), to revamp and coordinate the tours there. I was very excited about the possibilities and quickly volunteered for the position. As usual, Mrs. Stewart had words of warning for me but she was always eager to work with young people, which was what I loved most about her. I started at Tuff Gong on March 9, 2009.

From the onset, I realized that I had walked into a ticking time bomb. I felt like I was being rushed to produce results, which was certainly at odds with my calculating personality. On April 1, I made a note in a book that I used to keep track of my professional progress. It read: *"When art is rushed, it loses any chance at perfection; Tuff Gong, a location that should represent Bob Marley and his art the most, is being rushed after being allowed to decay over time; it should be allowed more time to grow than the deadlines that seem to appear out of thin air."*

Perhaps the problem was I all along. Anything that I felt strongly about, I approached that thing as a work of art. I loved Tuff Gong from the moment I became familiar with it and I always saw the potential for it to become the pride of Jamaica and a haven for youth in want and need of personal development. I wanted to make that happen as a direct result of my input, which was why the meager salary did not bother me much. I expected that, given a year to work at my own pace and enact my own plans, there would be tangible evidence to prove my effect on the company. It was the challenge that I relished, the preferred alternative to the mundane tour guiding at the already flourishing Museum. Tuff Gong was located in the realm of undesirability, below the Half Way Tree clock, and that was where I wanted to put my energy.

Even so, I was unhappy with the situation and, as always, I was willing to walk away from the thing I wanted most if I could not have it my way. The managing director, Stephanie Marley, made her displeasure clear and I agreed that I was not the man for the job. I was reinstated as a tour guide at the Museum as of April 6.

For the next two months or so, I was happy. Yes, the tour routine was mundane and annoying at times, and, yes, I often felt like a machine, but it was much less taxing on the brain than my stint at Monte Carlo. I was certain of that fact. Also, Mrs. Stewart always made an effort to spread positive vibrations among her staff while maintaining order as she saw fit. I thought it was a balance that only few people could achieve and I appreciated her for it. When I was not conducting a tour or eating lunch, I was usually reading a book or napping under the trees, hoping for the cool breeze that often made me feel blessed. In more talkative moods, I enjoyed lighthearted conversations mainly with the other tour guides and the tour supervisor, Miss Rowe. Once again, I was glad to be experiencing the very unique, mystical aura that existed at the Bob Marley Museum.

One day in May, I was enjoying a good book under the trees after my work shift had ended when I decided to rest my eyes for a while. I threw my head back onto the back of the bench where I sat and looked directly above at the leaves of a mango tree. I knew it as the tree along the tour route where we were supposed to pause and tell tourists that one of the large pictures of Bob Marley that adorned the wall next to the parking lot was taken there. As I stared at the leaves, I had an overwhelming feeling that a mango was somewhere beyond the leaves, out of my line of vision, and that it was going to fall directly on my head. At the time, many mangoes were ripening and falling off the trees on the compound, so it certainly was not impossible that one would fall in my vicinity. Still, the probability of a person pre-empting the descent of a mango from a tree onto his or her head at a precise moment was very slim. Yet, there I was with an almost absolute certainty that gravity intended to hit me with a Bombay mango. For roughly five more seconds I continued to stare upward, waiting for the deed to be done so that I could either catch or dodge the projectile. Momentarily, I speculated that I was going mad because my conviction was statistically at odds with mathematics. So I convinced myself to look away; I lowered my head and motioned to pick up my book or something else. Then, no later than two seconds after removing my gaze from the tree, it happened. I heard a snap and the rustling of the leaves above my head. Knowing what was taking place, I dared not look up for fruit to hit me in my face. I simply braced myself for the inevitable contact. The mango conked me on top of my head and landed on the white stones that layered the ground in front of the 'Black My Story' trailer. At that moment, two men who were conversing with each other out of earshot suddenly looked in my direction. One of them, a Rasta, exclaimed immediately to the other something to the effect of, "See it deh!" Apparently they were having a discussion of mystical proportions and the mango incident provided a great illustration of his point. I explained to the small gathering – Chicken was there too – that I knew the mango was going to hit me seconds before it happened. Everyone agreed that the mango belonged to me and that I better eat it, which was slightly odd to me because, generally, people immediately claimed fallen mangos at the Museum.

Blessings of that nature were not rare for me at 56 Hope Road so I was content to remain there until the time was right to go back to 220 Marcus Garvey Drive – Tuff Gong's street address. I'm not sure why I was so confident that I was going back there. It might have been because I read *Autobiography of a Yogi* by Paramahansa Yogananda during that time; it might have been because I was still involved with the development of the Tuff Gong tour script; or it might have been the simple reason that I loved Tuff Gong so much that I felt I had unfinished business there. Either way, I determined that patience was vital.

As fate would have it, I was asked to work five consecutive half-day shifts at Tuff Gong. I was there from Monday, May 18 to Friday, May 22, after which I returned to my regular shifts at the Museum. Before my departure though, I started to document some initial thoughts for resurrecting the Tuff Gong brand by connecting it to youth development and the re-emerging live music movement. By that time, I had been to two or three Jamnesia Sessions in Bull Bay with Oje and I was very enchanted by it. I knew that there was no better way to utilize Tuff Gong's diminishing resources than to align it with the movement that I observed as the right growth for the local music industry. It was very clear to me and I thought that Bob Marley himself most definitely would have wanted his company to play an integral role in the reconstruction of a damaged music industry. Therefore, back at the Museum, I asked Mrs. Stewart for her time one afternoon and told her in no uncertain terms that I wanted to go back to Tuff Gong; and in no uncertain terms, she told me that there was no chance of returning to the Museum after such a transfer. I realized that she was becoming impatient with me, as any reasonable manager would, but she continued to support my ambitions as long as I worked to her satisfaction. As always, I appreciated when she granted my request and authorized my second official appointment at Tuff Gong.

Some of my co-workers were perplexed as to why I wanted to be at Tuff Gong as opposed to the Museum. To them, it was a matter of being uptown, with better lunch options and many more tourists (thus, a better chance of receiving tips), versus being downtown, with its gloomy cloud of despair and depression. To me, it was a matter of where my energy and strategic mind would best serve humanity. That was downtown. The lunch situation did become a serious issue for me though, with no on-site restaurant and only one Rastafarian establishment providing substantial vegetarian meals in the Three Miles area – I was consciously attempting to eliminate meat from my diet by this time. The monotony of nutrition was bothersome and I sometimes did not eat well on the job but I found inspiration in the Bob Marley and the Wailers song, 'Them Belly Full,' particularly when I heard the line, "the rain ah fall but the dutty tough!'

Dutty was Tuff, indeed!

19
THE ELEMENTS

Mindful of my fortunate journey thus far, I was always reminding myself to be thankful for the quality of my existence. Financially, I had never been in possession of enough money to save for a rainy day, but I was always able to eat a meal and make small, affordable investments in pursuit of my mission. For instance, books were constant priorities and, if I could find the funds, I would buy something on the internet or link up with I-Nation, a real source of intellectual nourishment for revolutionaries living in Jamaica.

I gave thanks on an even deeper level as well. I had read *The Alchemist* by Paulo Coelho after receiving it from Gavin Sheppard in Toronto and I quickly recognized the truth in its assertion that the Universe consistently conspired to bring about the conditions necessary for a person to fulfill his or her destiny. My personal experiences were enough proof for me, and I could even recall a relevant example from when I was ten years old; an extraordinary thing happened to me then. It was 1993 and I was sleeping in my home at Forrest Hill Gardens. The alarm sounded on the kitchen radio and my mother started to get busy in the house as usual. She was going to wake me up in a short while so that I could begin preparing myself for school, but it wasn't a regular school day at all. It was the day that I would sit the

Common Entrance Examinations and that was a momentous occasion in the life of a Jamaican child. A good result on the Common Entrance usually meant one could attend the high school of one's choice; a less impressive score might be enough to get one into his or her "second choice" school; poor performance would probably result in repeating grade six or otherwise delaying the child's educational advancement. I usually achieved grades that were above average but that fact did not prevent me from being nervous. As I put on my uniform, the kitchen radio continued to blare with the sound of Francois St. Juste on FAME 95FM. He was infamous for his wake up call ("Gooooooooooooooooooooooood moooooooooooorniiiiiiiiiiing, Jaaaaaaaaaaamaaaaaaaaaaaaica!") and he did a very nice thing that morning. He dedicated a song to all the children who were about to take the exams. The song was 'Three Little Birds' by Bob Marley and the Wailers. By that time, I was standing by the front door, looking outside through the metal grill and wooden windowpanes. At that moment, song still playing and all, I saw three little birds. Not quite on my doorstep, the birds were actually resting on a power line across the street from my gate. When I looked at them and processed their existence at the precise moment when I was listening to Marley's voice, a tremendous calm swept through me. I went on to not only pass the Common Entrance, but to be accepted to attend my "first choice" high school and earn a scholarship from the Bank of Nova Scotia in the process. To know that, years later, I was instrumental in establishing the first *Africa Unite Youth Symposium* in Jamaica, and that I was subsequently employed at the record company founded by Bob Marley himself was nothing short of a blessing to me. I was consciously participating in my personal legend and that gave me the greatest joy I had ever known.

Since the Common Entrance, I conditioned myself to accept birds as signs and warnings but I was beginning to read other signs as well. After my first contract with the Bob Marley Foundation had ended, I had a very interesting conversation with a lovely woman who I knew as Queen Mother Nefertiti-El. Shortly before the Symposium, she was a guest on Mutabaruka's program, *The Cutting Edge* on IRIE FM. People called in to speak to her and listen to her tell them things of relevance to their lives. I initially thought it was a joke, to be honest, but I doubted that Mutabaruka would have risked his credibility to endorse somebody who did not exude authenticity in some way. Days later, I met her at Liberty Hall and I asked her to tell me something about myself. She looked at me with a warm smile and told me to ask her again another time. More than a week later, I went to the Museum, perhaps to collect money or some other reason, and I briefly stopped by the *Africa Unite* office to speak with some friends – I think my brethren Winston was there at the time. Queen Mother Nefertiti appeared in the doorway, looking for Mrs. Marley who was not yet there. As she turned to leave, I went after her and reminded her that she promised to speak to me. "Walk with me," she said, and the Career Book documents my highlights from the conversation.

At the museum, I spoke with Queen Mother Nefertiti-El. That was an enlightening conversation... she took a little time to tell me a bit about myself. Although I gave her a few clues about my intentions and mission, she ended up describing me very well. She called me "the whirlwind," with reference to Marcus Garvey.

Then, in the same entry, I mentioned a concept that was, until then, alien to my thought process.

She prays to the Earth, the oceans, the wind, the sun... she prays to nature... I like it. [February 15, 2008, 3:26am, CB]

It was a strange concept to say or hear out loud – "praying to nature" – but I immediately absorbed the implication of the Queen Mother's message. When that February 2008 conversation happened, I was already developing a certain reverence for the natural elements (which complemented my interest in Chinese philosophy). By the time I was working at Tuff Gong more than a year later, I had been conducting my own private studies of the yin-yang symbol and I was no longer reading just birds, but I was also opening myself up to learning lessons from the natural elements of fire, earth (the land, not the entire planet), water and air. As time went on, I discovered a special, sacred place for inspiration regarding each element.

The first element that I gravitated towards was fire, naturally, because my spirit had always been fiery and potentially explosive. The place where I focused most on fire was at the studio for the Uprising Roots Band, in the Windward Road area. The first time I visited, there was a fire burning, allegedly for months without being put out. The fire's custodian was Black Kush and I could see immediately that it was an important job that he approached with the utmost reverence and seriousness. It was certainly his most important contribution to my spiritual development. That fire consistently blessed me in almost unspeakable ways and my conversations with Kush helped me to grow into a greater overstanding of the eternal fire, the sun and the light energy that still exists in me today. At the Fire Base – the name I called it in honor of its meaning to my life – I also re-acquainted myself with somebody who I least expected to see again. Mama G, the maroon priestess, was often there and it brought me an immediate and unexplainable joy to see her again. I knew we were meant to be in proximity of each other for a greater purpose and I was eager to witness that destiny unfold.

The next center of elemental meditation was actually at Tuff Gong. At the end of the compound, next to the vinyl factory, there was a garden being tended to by a man called Humble. He was a Rasta who I met at 56 Hope Road when I was working on the Symposium. In his eyes I saw wisdom but I never got the chance to really develop a relationship with him until my reinstatement at Tuff Gong. There, Stephanie Marley was really trying to make the garden a part of the tour route and I liked the idea very much. The garden at the Museum was small and served more as an exhibit to be looked at and passed by, but the Tuff Gong Herbal Garden, which it was eventually advertised as, was an experience in and of itself. Tourists were able to walk through and touch and feel a wider variety of plants, and they could also sit on a bench and really absorb the natural mystic. It was certainly my favorite place to be during lunch breaks, especially when I needed to rejuvenate my soul before tackling the more mundane tasks associated with my work. Humble was a great philosopher, fittingly Rastafarian, and I loved to learn his wisdoms related to plants among other general discussions. In that garden, my Earth Base, I experienced new revelations that sharpened my intuitive senses. I also discovered the significance of the raven, a type of bird that I had not consciously observed until then.

My Water Base was a well known public attraction – Bath, St. Thomas. I loved going there with a small group of people, usually fellow young revolutionaries. It was important for many of us to wash off in the hot mineral water and I often went there a day or few before a major life challenge. At first, I didn't know that a challenging situation was approaching but, rather, I was feeling a heavy burden that made me welcome the idea of being in the presence of mineral water. Subsequently, I learned that the urge to visit the Water Base was connected to an impending, stressful life situation. The first time I went, Black Kush was our designated driver for the 2-hour journey each way. A more or less constant presence on my trips to Bath was Janine 'Jah9' Cunningham, a sister soldier who I met at the Fire Base. I immediately loved her energy as most people did and her companionship was very important to me. She could have given birth to my child (a general thought of mine whenever I considered the energy of any strong, conscious woman) or she could have been nothing more than a fellow revolutionary fighter in arms; the only consistent thought in my mind regarding her was that she was meant to have a great influence on my mission and the nature of that connection hardly mattered. At the Water Base, she was often the issuer of baptisms, in my mind, and I always appreciated the value of her actions in deliberately trying to strengthen everyone else around her. The Water Base was where I might have delved the deepest into myself, mostly because it was necessary. To withstand the initial pain caused by the hot water there, I had to either step outside of myself completely or go to a place within where I could disconnect from the sensory system of my body. Mentally, I was more prepared to attempt the latter strategy and, one night under the full moon, I did exactly that. I was amazed that I could achieve a mind state that was subconscious and simultaneously super conscious in my view. I never quite experienced it the same afterwards but I never lost the memory of it.

As for my meditations on air, I always had a fascination for that element. The birds might have had something to do with that fact or maybe my earliest indication was in 1988 when, without permission from my mother, I ran outside into the eye of Hurricane Gilbert (one of my most vivid childhood memories). Regardless, I always enjoyed reading the clouds. I usually saw human or animal faces; occasionally, I saw other shapes. I also loved to feel a breeze or observe the patterns of wind. In 2009, I had not yet discovered a place where I felt a particularly strong connection to that element, and it was not until the following year that I actually discovered a place that inspired me to call it my Air Base. One location that I really enjoyed though, as of September 2009, was Oje's new home in rural Saint Andrew, dubbed House of Diggy. By that time, I was very much in love with life and was practicing to find my center of inner balance. The Universe, personified, must have been satisfied with my progress because it obviously decided that it was time for a test of my patience.

On September 25, I was told that a man spoke on national radio telling his audience that he was appointed by God to do a radio show called 'Reasoning' and that it would begin in days. On September 27, there was a full-page advertisement on page 7 of the 'Sunday Finance' section of the Sunday Observer as well a half-page advertisement on the front page of the 'Arts & Education' section of the Sunday Gleaner. In both instances, there was an image of a bald-headed man with his arms folded. That man, who used to be dreadlocked, was the host-to-be of this new 'Reasoning' and his name was Dr. Leahcim Semaj. His name was significant for the simple reason that he had been a telephone guest on Reggie and my Reasoning, and he was a memorable one at that!

A year and a half prior, on March 12, 2008, we introduced Dr. Semaj on air during an episode discussing the phenomenon of "hustling." I usually tried to break the ice, so to speak, by saying something in jest to our guests so that they would recognize that our program incorporated light-heartedness and informal interactions. In the case of Dr. Semaj, I was quite intrigued by the fact that his name used to be Michael James and that he declared himself Leahcim Semaj by reversing the order of the letters. I decided, well in advance of show time, that I would try to have him speak about that before we discussed the night's topic with him. When I made mention of "Michael James" though, he made a witty retort and sidestepped the issue. I did not pursue it any further and laughed with the belief that he also found humor in our initial exchange, then we had our discussion and he went off air. I thought it was an average episode and I had moved on with my life mission thinking that the show went well. In fact, the Career Book has a March 14 entry in which I recorded my opinion that Semaj was *"a great telephone guest."* He, though, had seemingly been left with a negative feeling about the show. On a day following the airing, Reggie called Dr. Semaj to thank him for being a guest on Reasoning, as was routine for him to do with all our guests, but the routine phone call did not unfold as expected. Reggie later told me that Dr. Semaj was clearly upset at the young man who called him Michael James. In essence, how dare I call the man by his given name when he officially changed it himself? I resolved from that 2008 day that Semaj had an enormous ego and a pompous, perhaps holier-than-thou personality. Eighteen months later, the man was using the name 'Reasoning' for a program on Hot 102FM, five days (or 20 hours) per week. Given my growing knowledge of nature and the Universe, I found it extremely hard to believe that God told the guy to create a program with the same name as another one that left him with such egotistical trauma.

Semaj fancied himself a savior for Jamaica and his show began on September 28, 2009. We were off air for six months by then so we had no claim to the Reasoning name except for the sealed envelope that I mailed to myself when we conceptualized the program in 2007. We were advised against taking legal action, mostly because of the fact that our elders were generally more connected and there was enough corruption in Jamaican society to have any such endeavor be a general waste of our time and money. I had other ways in mind to shed light on the situation and possibly embarrass the man, but I decided, in the end, to focus on the blessings in my life. It was more important to continue building with Oje and advancing the Tuff Gong mission, while learning more lessons of peace from the natural elements, than to engage myself in a pointless battle for which I was probably not prepared. Around that time, I was told that Anthony Abrahams, Tony Shaw and Leahcim Semaj (probably as Michael James) were known to be chummy acquaintances for a long time. I believed it when I heard it and I treated that information like a vital piece of a puzzle. Even so, I decided to be patient, knowing that the Universe would take care of them accordingly.

For the rest of the year, I continued to work diligently at the corner of Marcus Garvey Drive and Bell Road. At times though, I felt like I was answering to too many different people within the Bob Marley Group – by that time, I was not only Tours Coordinator for Tuff Gong but also Communications Coordinator for the entire group, including Tuff Gong, Bob Marley Museum and Bob Marley Foundation. When the circumstances frustrated me on the job, I had another channel through which to exercise my self-determination. Supporting the career of Protoje was a blessing because, in that case, he was the only person who needed to approve my ideas, and that wasn't the only reason. More importantly, he had a very clear vision about where he was going and his confidence was such that he would tell me exactly what was required in the simplest terms. Anything extra was fluff to him, and he allowed me to provide that fluff at my own discretion, thus giving me a great avenue for self-expression. The best example of this occurred at his December 4 stage show, *The Seven Year Wish*, which happened precisely when we planned it to happen (just like every other of the year's objectives that we discussed in January). There, I was tasked to be the master of ceremonies for the presentation and his requirements were minimal. We did not rehearse anything regarding what I would say. He simply gave me ample warning and provided me with any information that he thought I needed or that I otherwise requested. Like me, he seemed to believe in the adage, "what will be, will be," and had enough confidence in himself to trust that all would unfold the way it should. *The Seven Year Wish* was a great example of an organic production and I was able to express myself in the process. It remains one of my fondest memories to date, regardless of any flaws that I perceived in my own contribution.

I also reconnected with Che towards the end of 2009. He was ready to expand the Manifesto movement to Jamaica and wanted us to start building a team. We immediately got Reggie involved, and then Lesley, who included some of her colleagues. The first official Manifesto|Jamaica meeting took place in November with Lesley, Kareece Lawrence, Natalie Reid (who hosted the meeting at her home), Donisha Prendergast (Rita and Bob Marley's granddaughter) and me. Before the end of the year, we had a nice outdoor meeting close to my home with a larger contingent. There, Maria Hitchins first suggested the use of the word "art'ical" as a buzzword to associate with the movement. We immediately loved it and I think that was the day when we successfully energized a critical number of core members to move Manifesto|Jamaica forward at the rate required to make it happen.

On the last night of the year, some members of the newly formed Manifesto|Jamaica team went on a trip to Bath, my Water Base. On the way there, I felt very optimistic about the upcoming year and I was happy to be in good company. Many of the people who became the driving force of Manifesto|Jamaica were some of Taiwo's closest friends - the Bebble Rock team - and I could not help but remember how seriously he urged me, less than three years before, not to stop pursuing my goal. On the way back home, on the first morning of the new year, I felt like a noticeably evolving being, like my intuitive powers were fully charged and I was ready to unlock the next level of my spiritual growth.

2010

20
ISM, NO SCHISM

On the second day of 2010, I was finally ready to do something that I constantly imagined for the previous year and a half: maintain a blog. It was a fairly natural progression for a person whose main preoccupation was writing but the idea and motivation was born out of special circumstances. Shortly before going to Toronto, IdlerzLounge.com was hacked. Not only was that a breach of my website's security and the security of its members but, in a way, it was also a breach of my personal security. That event triggered a series of thoughts in my mind, eventually culminating in a new resolution, which was that I would begin to focus more on developing myself before overindulging in my efforts to uplift society. I knew that my vision for IL was grand and seemingly insurmountable, especially given the fact that most of its members did not see things the way I did. Therefore, I determined that the most progressive approach to making significant strides in my lifetime was to solidify my own convictions and, in that way, attract more people with similar thoughts and revolutionary intentions. By then, I was happy to have met a few likeminded people as a direct result of speaking my mind on nationally syndicated radio and at Liberty Hall. Soon, I was going to express myself in Toronto and expand the circle of influence. I grew to overstand the laws of attraction and I wanted the momentum to continue, so I registered the website, Duttyism.com, knowing that the strength of my writing eclipsed the potency of my oratory skills. I wanted to experience a segment of my personal growth in public view, which I did on Reasoning but never completely on my own terms and at my own pace.

Since then, I was trying to develop ideas for what the website would look like, even working on ideas for a logo. I recall that Froggy drew a sketch of a hybrid animal that was a dog with the tail of a scorpion, representing the combination of my Chinese and Western zodiac signs. For whatever reason though, the Universe was not inspiring me to write anything that I thought aligned with my vision for Duttyism.com and I allowed the domain to sit undeveloped for many months until I found the right inspiration. Then, Carl Jung and Malidoma Patrice Some made two very important contributions to my meditation in 2009 – *Psychology and Alchemy* and *Of Water and the Spirit* respectively. I was led to the first book after I started visualizing a symbol in my mind; it was a simple symbol involving a triangle and a circle but it potentially had varying implications, depending on the way I looked at it. Well, on the day when the mango fell on my head at the Museum, I put that mango in my bag to eat it later and then forgot about it. That night, I went to the Fire Base and, while there, a feeling of hunger swept through my stomach. I usually endured such hunger until I went home but I was pleased when I remembered the mango. I reached into my bag, took it out, and then felt like I wanted to be alone with it. After all, the mango chose me! So, I walked a little bit away from the fire and noticed the moon, which shone a strong beam of light in a particular area. I decided that I wanted to eat my mango in that beam of moonlight and it was precisely in that spot where an object rested on the ground. When I inspected the object, I saw the unmistakable symbol of the circle and the triangle and, from then on, I knew the right way to look at the symbol. My studies of that symbol led me to seek Jung's book, which was bought for me by my sister, Golda.

Some's book was another gift given to me in November 2009, and I finished reading it shortly before my extraordinary experience at the Water Base on New Year's Eve. By then, I was again making an effort to launch Duttyism.com and, on January 2, 2010, with Smitty's assistance, I launched my blog with a simple design and a few words that I posted deliberately to set the tone. I wanted people to know that I was doing it for myself but also for the benefit of those who had an urge to develop themselves and be confident in their own personal philosophies. I knew, from the start, that what I was venturing to do would not give me widespread popularity and I was comfortable with that knowledge. I was writing for the benefit of future generations and did not mind that people of my own generation might possibly consider me to be insane. My comfort was always in the fact that people, such as Marcus Garvey, were initially disregarded and faced greater tribulations than me. Truth always revealed itself in due time and, like Fidel Castro, I always felt that history would absolve me. I wrote on my blog like my life depended on my honesty, and continue to approach it with that mentality today.

Ten days after the launch of Duttyism.com, a terrible earthquake in Haiti left devastation in its wake. At first, it affected me like it did most people in Jamaica. I recognized the suffering of our Black human siblings who were already struggling in the post-colonial world. Then, after a few more days, I started to go through a profound psycho-spiritual change. It began on January 16, a Saturday.

I was reasoning with Reggie at a quiet location and I was in a militant mood. I told him that we had to carefully study the lessons of the most notable and relevant leaders before us because they left their wisdoms for us to learn and continue the mission. It was a very powerful conversation of the variety that I often had with Reggie and not many other people. At the time, there were some ravens resting in our vicinity and I also counted eleven of them that flew above our heads. That signaled something special to me and I wondered what the birds knew about me or us. I went to Jamnesia that night.

The next day, I felt like being at the Fire Base, where I did not generally visit on many Sundays. On that occasion, Black Kush, Mama G and Jah9 were there and I was partaking in a steam chalice, which contained a particularly agreeable strain of herbs. Soon, I was reading the clouds and saw what appeared to be a crescent moon. It struck me as noteworthy because I usually saw faces. Then, at nearly that exact moment, a random thought flew into my mind: "I am Dutty Bookman. The same man who started the Haitian Revolution is me."

There was no traceable train of thought that led to that declaration. It simply happened with suddenness and unexplainable clarity. I knew that it was true and I believed it with all my being. As soon as I experienced the fullness of the thought, a framed image of Haile Selassie I, which Black Kush kept next to the fire (and attached to his drum set during his performances), suddenly fell face down! I was shocked and I immediately blurted out the words, "Selassie drop!" Beside me, Jah9 was sitting and, as the steam chalice passed between us, she quietly said something to the effect of, "Him never drop. Him ah bow to you." She was known to say profound things like that and make me (and others) feel confident and powerful. That was one of my favourite things about her. Those words were unforgettable though, due to the fact that I had a certain thought in my head at the precise moment when Selassie "bowed to me." The wind started to pick up at that moment, and swirled around and around – a noticeable whirlwind. Also, a picture of Marcus Garvey (who is known to have said, "look for me in the whirlwind...") was placed at the fireside for the first time on that day, simply because Kush, I assumed, was inspired to put it there through his own connection with the Universe. The combination of all these seemingly random and isolated events into one major moment of relevance to me was what made me know that the Universe was validating my newfound conviction; I was being reassured that I was on the right track. I went into a blissful meditation at that point and three birds appeared on the guinep tree that hovered over the fire. From that day forth, I realized that everything was going to be all right, just as Bob Marley had sung. Over the next few days, I experienced profound revelations, every single day. I expressed many of them to a few persons as soon as I experienced them, mostly because I was so overwhelmed that I needed to speak to people who I felt were trustworthy; today, I'm not so quick to speak about everything that happened during those days. Despite that, there are some incidents that I wish to be documented in this text.

On Tuesday, January 19, I attended one of a series of ongoing meetings at the Museum to plan the Bob Marley Earthday celebrations. As I was parking the car, which my mother had loaned me after she bought herself a new one, an interesting feature was being aired on Bess FM. I was being discussed on national radio (which is to say that the Haitian Revolution icon, Dutty Boukman was being discussed). I sat in the car for a few minutes, absorbing some new information about my previous incarnation that I had not yet learned. Only after the feature was done did I turn off the car and go to the meeting; I was a little late due to my necessary delay but the meeting did not start yet in any case. That day, I picked up a brethren called Trevor, who worked at the Museum, at a bus stop across the road and he insisted that I carry an old lady as well. Only after we drove off did I realize that he was not related to her and had just met her at the bus stop. I was happy to converse with her anyway and she gave me a very warm feeling. After dropping off Trevor somewhere around Half Way Tree, I dropped off the elder at the intersection of Hagley Park Road and Waltham Park Road on my way to Tuff Gong. She left me with the energy of her wisdom, which added to my day's meditation on the feminine aspects of existence. After parking the car, I was walking toward the vinyl factory when I saw Joavan 'Yagga' Puran, a Rasta youth who did a lot of the visual artwork at Tuff Gong, including paintings on the outside wall as well as fresh versions of the company's logo at the parking lot and by the factory. As I approached him, I saw that he had made a lot of progress painting a wall that had been plain the day before. A part of his mural included the lyrics to Ziggy Marley's 'Beautiful Mother Nature' and I experienced a very soft emotion as soon as I witnessed Yagga's art. That night,

I went home and meditated in such a way that I imagined myself transported to the core of the Earth. Since then, I have not experienced anything like that to date.

The next day, Wednesday, January 20, was mostly uneventful. I actually thought that my mystical experiences were over and I was beginning to relax because, by then, I was worried about my sanity. Little did I know, it was only a short break in the scheme of things. After regular work hours ended, I stayed in office in order to get more work done, since I had been so shaken by my recent revelations that I was not being very efficient during the days that week. Unfortunately, the overtime attempt was unsuccessful on that first night because something very strange happened on the computer at my desk. At least, it was unexplainable to the extent of my knowledge of computer systems and it led me to a conversation with Imani Wilmot, otherwise called SoulKisser, the daughter of the legendary Reggae artist and Jamnesia founder, Billy 'Mystic' Wilmot. The young lady became a fast friend of mine in 2009 and I found her to be a very intriguing individual. Our friendship was not one characterized by frequent contact but she was always timely in speaking to me. Through her, the Universe communicated many important things to me and, during those monumental days of January 2010, she was a source of encouragement for me. After our discussion that evening, I was motionless at my desk for a while and decided to give up on any chance of accomplishing the work that I intended to do that evening. After clocking out, I noticed the moon on my way to the parking lot, it was in the crescent phase, or almost a quarter phase, and I recalled the cloud shape that I saw at the Fire Base days earlier. I drove to Stagga's place that evening and socialized with him, Oje, Reggie and some other people. On my way home after that, I was giving Reggie a ride to his abode when I noticed that the same crescent moon, which was high in the sky and radiantly white when I saw it at Tuff Gong, was currently very low and duller and much more yellow, even tending towards a shade of orange. I was on Washington Boulevard at the time and I drove into the parking lot of the Jamaica Baptist Union in an attempt to video record the moon with my cell phone. I was displeased with the quality and gave up quickly, then we resumed our journey westward on the boulevard with the moon almost directly ahead of us, although slightly to the right. When I dropped Reggie at his gate and started to drive off towards my home, I turned up the volume on the radio, which was muted due to the fact that I was reasoning with Reggie throughout the journey. Upon applying the volume, I realized that the radio was tuned in to *The Cutting Edge* on IRIE FM. A song was playing and I must have liked its vibration because I continued listening, soon to hear lyrics referring to me (Boukman). Then, Mutabaruka's voice began to speak about Boukman and I drove the whole way home barely paying attention to the roads before me. I listened to him intently up until I parked the car, at which point he finished his speech about the subject – perfect timing. I shut off the car and made my way indoor. That night, I noticed that the moon had transitioned from an orange to a deep, blood red in color. The next morning, I described the moon that I saw to Yagga, who then said to me, matter-of-factly, "Voodou moon, yeah." I was mid-sentence when I heard it and had to stop myself to ask him to repeat what he said. Those were the words that brought me over the edge. I had never heard of a Voodou moon before then but I knew that the Universe was, again, speaking to me through the lips of another human being, just like it did with so many others. They may not have understood why they said the things they said to me, or they may have had one intention while leaving me with a different impression; the important thing was that I understood why the Universe was allowing the discourse to occur. Speaking to Yagga at that moment, I immediately found the relevance: a so-called Voodou moon was witnessed on a night when I so happened to listen to a radio program that was speaking about Boukman, who was a houngan (or Voodou priest), the same Boukman who, on the same occasion when I read a crescent moon in the clouds, I intuitively felt was a previous incarnation of my own spirit. I didn't need any more signs at that point. In fact, I could barely withstand the rate of the revelations any longer and I became very emotional.

That morning, as I sat down at my desk, I realized that I was not going to get a lot of work done with so much on my mind. I knew that the Bob Marley Earthday celebrations were approaching and I needed to perform optimally or not at all. As I soaked it all in, Lorna 'Sister Lorna' Wainwright walked by my desk and must have noticed that something was bothering me; she asked me if I was okay. Initially, I answered affirmatively but I knew that I would tell her eventually. Sister Lorna was a guardian angel at Tuff Gong. As Operations Manager, she was a stern, authority figure who, behind the occasional scolding, was also a very loving individual. I knew from the first time I met her in person – February 6, 2009 with the Project Nine Mile crew – that she was a good, motherly companion and the glue holding Tuff Gong together. When I first worked at Tuff Gong, she went on vacation and didn't return until after I was transferred back to the Museum. It was upon my return to Tuff Gong that I got to know her better and I loved being in the company of her and Kim Daley from the accounting department. On another level, I discerned that Sister Lorna had a very important role in carrying out the will of the Universe. I particularly related to her story about how she started working at Tuff Gong. In summary, she had difficulties finding a job with her dreadlocks as a young woman and Bob Marley, who saw her looking depressed one day, asked her what was the problem. She told him about her dilemma after which Brother Bob replied that he was going to establish a record company so that Rasta people could work, and that she could work for him. Her subsequent path led her to a desk at 220 Marcus Garvey Drive and my path led me to a desk beside hers. On that January 2010 morning, Voodou moon and all, I indicated to Sister Lorna that I needed to talk to her in the Herbal Garden right away and I walked to the end of the compound into the security and comfort of my Earth Base. Shortly afterwards, Sister Lorna arrived with frankincense and myrrh in her possession and she lit them as I told her about my situation. I was very impressed with her intuition, as I had not given any impression of mysticism before I walked out of the office building. Again, I knew that the Universe was in control of our actions. Our conversation that day was a very natural progression and felt like the way things were meant to be. Following our conversation, Sister Lorna gave to me some of the frankincense and myrrh that she did not burn and then encouraged me to get back to work. I felt better but I still didn't know how I was going to manage myself that day, especially because, at about midday or so, I was scheduled to be a judge for the inaugural Bob Marley Debate Competition at the Louise Bennett Garden Theatre; I had already judged at least two such matches by that time and I knew that it required my focus. Thankfully, the Universe was sympathetic to my needs and really wasn't going to give me more than I could bear. On my way to the venue, one of the organizers called me to say that the match was no longer going to happen. I was relieved and decided to claim the rest of the Thursday for personal use. Later that evening, I went to the Fire Base, where Mama G told me that the Bookman of the 18th century, before he left Jamaica to go to Haiti, was originally from her particular Maroon town. I don't recall that she ever told me the name of the area where she was from, or maybe she said the name to me and I didn't listen or properly commit it to memory, but, whatever the case, I was fully absorbing her significance in my life. I wondered if she knew that I was the reincarnation of Dutty Bookman and if she was simply waiting for me to discover the fact on my own. Did she know who I was before I knew myself, back in February 2008 when she asked me for a copy of my speech at Liberty Hall? My name was publicized as Gavin Hutchinson at that symposium; there was no obvious reason for her to associate me – this short, light-skinned, uptown-raised, formally educated youth – with her revered ancestor who was known to be a tall, dark and menacing product of slavery. What parts of my speech could have provided her with a confirmation, or even a clue, that this Gavin person was actually Dutty? I have perplexed myself over that question many times, and I considered asking her related questions but habitually stopped myself from doing so when I had the chance. What I knew, regardless, was that my path and hers were purposefully interconnected.

The mystical revelations continued for some more days after that conversation but, today, I consider Wednesday and Thursday, January 20 and 21, to be the peak of the sustained activity that lifted me to a higher state of consciousness. I suddenly had a lot more to express on Duttyism.com than I had previously imagined. It was time for revolution once again, and this time my spirit was called upon to do what it did best: instigate something historic.

21
LIGHT OF THE TRINITY

My time spent at Tuff Gong remains a treasured memory. It is hard to describe the fullness of what it meant to be there during the days and to have some influence during that critical stage of its resurgence. The year before I was transferred there, while I was in Toronto, I walked into a shoe store and, as soon as I stepped inside, I noticed a shoe that seemed more illuminated than the others. Essentially, it called me and I walked directly to it, picked it up and purchased a pair. It was a special edition Tuff Gong design by Adidas, and they became my official "Gideon Boots." I wore them for any type of occasion: I wore them to casual events; I wore them to formal events; I wore them when I was exploring nature, through bushes and by many rivers; I wore them when I addressed the United States official during *Ignite The Americas*; I wore them when I was charged for possession of marijuana; I wore them when I spoke to Judy, the judge (in addition to a t-shirt with the symbol of a marijuana leaf on it); I had them on in the jail cell; I wore them as I walked the streets and rode the buses and robot taxis of Kingston. It stands to reason, then, that I wore the Gideon Boots to work, where I also often wore the "Sleeve of Justice," a military jacket that I purchased from an army store in Daytona Beach. Over time, I added various patches to it and it was undoubtedly one of my favorite charms. It was named during the 2007 hike in Saint Mary, when I experienced my first conscious recognition of the will of the Universe. My companions on that hike called it the Sleeve of Justice because, as we were following certain paths, I was using my arms to move thorny plants out of our way. I immediately loved the name and decided to keep referring to the jacket as such. Since then, the Sleeve of Justice had been my faithful companion, also present on many of the same journeys as the Gideon Boots.

I appreciated that I could dress comfortably at Tuff Gong. That made it easier for me to be productive and I made my presence there count towards the mission I felt had to be fulfilled. Stephanie Marley, Mrs. Stewart and Sister Lorna were the usual sources of direction for many of my accomplishments but I also injected my energy more enthusiastically into the projects that were aligned with my vision. From the beginning of my tenure, practically, I made it clear to management that I was most interested in making Tuff Gong more welcoming to youth artists and to the live music movement. One day, in the summer of 2009, I walked into the Rehearsal Studio for the first time. I was impressed by its good condition and equally astonished that it was constantly kept locked. Thereafter, I wanted management to decide on a cheap hourly rate for young people, especially those who lived in the surrounding inner city communities, to be able to use the space. I got approval to promote it but the actual rate that was agreed on was slightly prohibitive based on my research. I invited Maria Hitchins, Peter Abrikian and other young leaders in the arts and other fields to see the Rehearsal Studio with their own eyes. I also showed it to Janine and Oje, and started to spread the word through channels intended to alert students at the Edna Manley College of the Visual and Performing Arts. The most common complaint was the location; the second most common complaint was the price, but usually in relation to the location. Anywhere below the Half Way Tree clock was usually a problem for persons based uptown, meanwhile many persons based downtown simply could not afford the rate.

I also worked to re-stock the Record Shop with some new merchandise, mostly tourist gift items. That was largely a distraction for me and I eventually asked to be relieved of that responsibility. The act of conducting a tour also forced me to leave my desk when I was trying to accomplish other tasks but I mostly enjoyed interacting with the tourists. Unlike a majority of the tourists at the Museum, for example, people who visited Tuff Gong were more independent travelers who, like me, were hardly interested in sticking to the route prescribed by the major tour companies. They were normally intelligent conversationalists and lovers of Reggae music to the extent that they would teach me a few things. I especially loved to tour groups of school children. They were mostly well behaved and full of innocent expressions, with the exception of one or two high school groups, and I usually felt happier after basking in their energies.

Apart from that, my usual routine involved supporting the development of the websites, updating the blogs and promoting Tuff Gong's *Making of Music Tour*. On October 15, 2009, I did a memorable interview on TVJ's Smile Jamaica program, where I had fun discussing the nature of the tour with the hosts. Then, as February approached, my working world, of course, increasingly revolved around the Bob Marley Earthday celebrations. In my capacity as Communications Coordinator for the Bob Marley Group of Companies, I had to attend the planning meetings at the Museum, which often took me away from my work at Tuff Gong, where we were working towards launching the new Berhane Selassie Art Gallery. That was a project with which I was happy to be involved.

Stephanie Marley herself put forth the notion of an art gallery on Tuff Gong's compound. She had a decent art collection, wanted to display them and that combination of factors seemed to have been the motivation for clearing out a building that was being used as a storage facility. I was elated and applauded her foresight. When I learned that it was to be named in honor of Bob Marley, using his Ethiopian Orthodox Church baptismal name, Berhane Selassie, I found that very agreeable to my soul. Berhane Selassie means "light of the trinity," and, indeed, I perceived art as illumination in dark times. So, as February 2010 approached, I did what I could under the circumstances to launch the gallery successfully and to also position it as a platform for young people to gain exposure.

The launch went very well on February 3, 2010. The keynote speaker for the event was Jamaica's tourism minister, whose speechwriter ensured that he said the right things. After the cutting of the ribbon, we invited guests to view the art inside the gallery, which included pieces by two young Jamaican artists. The first was Laura-Anne Fung, whose work had appeared in a newspaper and subsequently caught Stephanie's eye. The second was Yagga, whose portrait of Haile Selassie I was a big hit; the tourism minister declared that he wanted to buy it (although he never did so, to my knowledge). Yagga's mural, the one that moved me so deeply when I first saw it in January, also adorned one of the outside walls of the gallery itself. After the formalities, I gave the tourism minister a complimentary tour, which could still be considered a formality. I tried to bring his attention to a stalk of cannabis on display in the Herbal Garden but he displayed a great proficiency in pretending not to hear me or notice the herb. At the end of the festivities, Miss Marley was very happy. In fact, I had never seen her hug so many people and I was surprised when she embraced me as well.

In my bid to use the gallery to expose youth artists, I have to admit that I fell drastically short of that goal. I lobbied management to launch an initiative that I conceived, tentatively called 'Project: Mural' or 'Mission: Mural' and aimed at attracting street artists (or graffiti artists) to submit visual art interpretations of Bob Marley and the Wailers songs. There was a long wall that stretched from the gate and almond tree next to the vinyl factory to the Herbal Garden; I figured that there was more than ample space to paint a few murals on the inside of it after selecting the most interesting interpretations. Some interpretations that were not selected for the wall would then be displayed in the Berhane Selassie Art Gallery. I was very excited about creating this avenue of exposure, and possible income, for talented, young people. I narrowed down the song titles that I preferred to be interpreted, avoiding the most popular ones like 'One Love' and opting for others like 'Zion Train,' which I felt had more relevance to Tuff Gong as an entity. I also worked assiduously to develop the application forms and guidelines. As February drew near though, I had to admit that I could not comfortably launch the project at the gallery launch ceremony, which was my original intention. So, I asked for an extension of a couple weeks and eventually completed my objective closer to the end of February, submitting my progress to the relevant people. Then, I waited.

Apart from the launching of the gallery, which was cause enough for celebration, February 2010 gave me another reason to celebrate. I further discovered my increased capacity to love my enemies, or, rather, those I perceived to be my enemies at the time. Two interesting things happened to prove this.

In promoting the schedule of Bob Marley Group activities, I made various appearances in mainstream media houses, including CVMTV, Irie FM and Roots 96.1FM. The one that I relished most was Hot 102FM, not for any special reason except that the particular program that I spoke on was the imitation 'Reasoning' that was hosted by Leahcim Semaj. I was happy to sit face-to-face with Dr. Semaj, figuring that he had little clue about the young man with whom he was conversing. It was an outside broadcast on the grounds of 56 Hope Road – my turf – and he was busy stuffing his face with his lunch while I spoke mainly to his co-host, a lovely lady whose name has since slipped me. It was all too easy for me to mention my background in radio as well as the fact that Semaj was a guest on my program of the same name, especially when the lady was so captivated by the fact that I studied rocket science that she insisted on a tangential discussion about my personality. I visualized a Semaj in shock, spitting out his mouthful of food, or choking on it, at the exposition of his immorality. Oh, what a day February 4, 2010 could have been! As I looked at him though, I realized that he was a pitiful sight in that moment. He was a human being of a different generation with a different mentality. He and people like him, including people of my own generation who blindly emulated our elders without seeking to improve things, were practically extinct without realizing or coming to terms with the fact. I decided to love him; I smiled with him and I finished the interview and I shook his hand and I walked away.

Six days after being within point blank range of that man who offended me, I spent hours celebrating with a brand that offended the entire nation. On February 10, 2010, I testified on film on behalf of Red Stripe's 'Project Artist,' a program aimed at developing young people within the music industry. One of its features was to pair each young person with a local company in an internship scenario and I think the Bob Marley Group accepted four such interns, two at the Museum and two at Tuff Gong. They started in December 2009 and switched locations in January to the best of my recollection. I mostly interacted with two of them: Ikanji and Imru. Ikanji in particular was the nephew of Senya, who, according to my research, might have been the first person to record a song inside the Tuff Gong studio when it was first established at 56 Hope Road; information suggested that Aston 'Family Man' Barrett tested out the new equipment with her, producing 'Children of the Ghetto,' which happened to be the ring tone on my cell phone when I met Ikanji. I found both him and Imru to be very enthusiastic and appreciative of Red Stripe's role in their lives. I, myself, also grew to recognize the value of the initiative, even if I thought that Diageo was still doing damage control after being at odds with the dancehall industry.

On that February morning, when a film crew showed up at Tuff Gong to interview Mrs. Stewart and me about the greatness of Project Artist, I decided to do it although I was at liberty to decline. My motivation that day, again, involved the fact that I wanted to show love. Red Stripe was trying to evolve with the times, albeit after public opinion forced them to do so, and they suffered from some of the same generational symptoms on an organizational level as Semaj did on an individual level. I just had to love them and focus on the Project Artist initiative, which was a positive act of creation. Later that evening, I also attended the graduation ceremony for the participants, held at the Jamaica Pegasus Hotel. There, I saw much of the expected gallivanting by local celebrities and I managed myself in that environment better than I had anticipated.

After the frantic rush of February, things generally slowed down at the office and I continued promoting the *Making of Music Tour* and the Berhane Selassie Art Gallery. In March, Empress Mullings and Steven Golding hosted their NewsTalk 93FM program, *The Corner*, at Tuff Gong, mostly at my insistence to management. My aim was to leverage their perceived popularity to attract the nearby inner city residents to the compound. That turned out to be an embarrassment for me, and a vast waste of resources for Tuff Gong, as it seemed like nobody in those inner cities listened to that program during the weekdays of March 22 to 26. That or the program did not have the gravitational pull that it appeared to tout. I rather enjoyed being in the company of the hosts though, and I was very happy when Humble spoke to them on air about the Herbal Garden.

I took some vacation time in April and, upon my return to office, Mission: Mural was still not advanced in any way since the time I had submitted my contribution two months prior. I was asked to resend the documents and I did so at the end of the month. Meanwhile, I was unofficially offered the position of Marketing Manager for the Bob Marley Group, pending a discussion with a director, and I agreed to it on the basis that I would also receive an increased salary. After the director was consulted, I was told that, although she approved of me assuming the Marketing Manager title, she did not believe I was being utilized enough to receive a pay raise. That news was not only contradictory but it also shocked me because I knew that I was being stretched thin in both a mental and physical sense. That event officially signaled the dusk of my motivation.

Before I resigned from the Bob Marley Group, I was already thinking about the next phase of its growth. I determined that the Bob Marley Museum had to become a venue of choice for the live music movement and that Tuff Gong must continue on a path towards becoming an incubator for young people. I pushed these ideas constantly in my conversations with Mrs. Stewart because I found her to be a forward thinking elder who aspired to leave the best possible legacy of contributions for future generations to build upon. Months later, as I witnessed the surge of events taking place at 56 Hope Road, and even one promising event at 220 Marcus Garvey Drive, I found myself wishing that I could have been a part of that unfolding. My comfort has since been in the fact that I played a vital and privileged role in turning on the switch for the Light of the Trinity, which will symbolically and actually benefit others. I was the man for that particular job and I did it successfully.

22
DETACHMENT

For a long time before I resigned from my job, I was preparing to move out of Carrol's place and find my own space to control. Reggie had a similar mindset and we therefore decided to actively seek somewhere to share. We soon found out that Froggy, who was already living with two other housemates, was getting ready to make another transition and was interested in building with us. I say "building" because we were expressly seeking a home that was conducive to revolutionary creativity; and we would know it when we saw it. Not long after Froggy joined the cause, we learned that a good brethren named Neville Ewers was also interested in finding a zone to build. I was extremely excited about the prospect of living under the same roof with these three industrious men but it turned out that I was way too busy with work (and was constantly tired as a result) to actively peruse the classified ads for rental homes. Reggie assumed the responsibility, more or less, and we looked at a few locations over a relatively long period of time. Then, in March 2010, as I was enjoying one of those Sundays of doing absolutely nothing, Reggie contacted me to say that he saw two promising options. Very reluctantly, I drove to pick him up and we went directly to the first place, off of Roehampton Drive. It seemed like a grand waste of time and gas, and I was apprehensive about going to the second place, which was in Armour Heights, a hill above the Manor Park area. Reggie insisted that he had a very good feeling about it and that it was basically the one that he was really looking forward to seeing. On the phone, the owner told him that there was no number on the gate but we were to look for three lions. Sure enough, we arrived to see a gate adorned with one majestic lion along with two other militant lions. Easily excitable by nature, I started exclaiming my choice "claat" at the sight of the lion statues. We parked and greeted the owner, a no nonsense Rasta man, who walked ahead of us, leading us to the front door of the vacant section of the house; he occupied an adjoining section and we were soon informed that a tenant lived in a separate room at the back of the large structure that we were about to enter. As we approached the front door, the movement of a pigeon, perched on a ledge above, drew my attention. As soon as I saw the bird, I knew that I was supposed to live there. The rest of the process was, simply, formality. We followed the owner inside and the place was very attractive. Likewise, the backyard was quaint and beautiful. I had seen enough. We later informed Froggy about the 3-bedroom gem that we discovered; by then, we learned that Neville was no longer prepared for the transition with us. We visited a second time with Froggy and, that day, informed the owner that we were going to rent.

A few days later, Froggy delivered the unfortunate news that his reservations were outweighing his desire to move to the place we quickly dubbed '3 Lionz'; suddenly, it was only Reggie and I caught in a commitment. The rent was quite steep, especially when only split two ways but we were both adamant about going there. By then, the bird on the ledge was no longer a factor in my mind as much as the fact that I was willing to run any risk in order to continue building with Reggie, especially a Reggie who made up his mind about something. From my point of view, I could almost see the vision in the very eyes of Marcus Garvey's reincarnation and I was not going to let him down. Therefore, we made plans to move in at the beginning of April, when I would use some of my vacation days from Tuff Gong, and to suffer any financial consequences in our bid to make revolutionary progress. I was certain that no other two persons, with bank accounts and income streams that resembled ours, would have decided to move into that house, but I decided to sideline my fears and focus on making it work. In my estimation, we needed to endure only about half a year of discomfort before we could advance our mission, whatever that was shaping up to become. Around that time, I had started to market my own writing services and was confident that I would be able to build up a comfortable base of clients in due time. We were also about to get knee deep in the work of Manifesto|Jamaica, which soon got off to a literally explosive start.

On Sunday, May 23 (Labour Day), we were at our first officially supported Manifesto|Jamaica event with tent and banner and all. It was a sports day for the Three Miles Development Area, an association with which we formed one of our earliest relationships, and a lot of different communities in the area were represented. There were especially a lot of children there. I was supposed to lead the halftime show (which was delayed almost to the very end of the event) on behalf of Manifesto|Jamaica, and was very excited about it, but I had to learn midway through the proceedings that I was not very good at creating the sort of excitement needed for the occasion. Luckily, Maria was there to see it through to the end and I was very happy about that. Approaching the end of the festivities, gunshots were heard a short distance away from the field of activity, signaling to us the beginning of the government operation to extradite Christopher 'Dudus' Coke. As negative acts of war were happening so close to us, the Manifesto|Jamaica team played a vital role in keeping the children occupied and focused on positivity and we otherwise assisted in a safe evacuation process. I have often reflected on that occasion as the real reason for Dudus' sacrifice. Stemming from political aggression from the United States government (and compliance by the Jamaican government), the conviction of Manifesto|Jamaica grew to not only repeat a catchy slogan and mission statement but, out of necessity, to really work to uplift as many young people as possible through arts and culture. From that day onward, we started to be the change that we wanted to see.

The situation with the halftime show was only the first of a few Manifesto|Jamaica related instances when I would commit to something and not see it through to the end. The fact was that I was becoming very detached from the pulse of things, as I had been living it since my triumphant return to Jamaica in 2006. All of a sudden I was approaching 28-years-old and feeling more exhausted than my age implied I should. The more I tried to do, the less it seemed I could bear to do. It did not take long for me to declare the things that I would not do instead of the things I would, and I started to focus on my real singular contribution to the revolution that was taking place. I was a writer, not necessarily the organizer or public speaker of my fantasies. I was an adjusted version of the legendary Boukman, the man who was an avid reader. Like him, I had been a modern day house negro, rubbing shoulders with some of society's so-called distinguished personalities; additionally, I was not only fond of absorbing information, but I was also a highly proficient writer and, thus, an effective disseminator of information. It was my duty to write the revolution and so I did. Everything else that I previously committed to had to be picked up by others and I had faith that the Universe was going to align everybody's energies according to its will. In the process, I was altering the state of some of my most valued friendships and became practically estranged from some of the people for whom I felt great affection. My saving grace during that difficult period was 3 Lionz.

Yes, upon that hill I learned some of the most valuable lessons about myself. In due time, I became conscious of the fact that my new home was, in truth, my Air Base. It was the last element for me to include in my deepest meditative states, as I already knew the relevance of fire, water and earth to my life. The Fire Base was where I first realized that my fiery spirit could be controlled as a steady flame, supplying warmth instead of being allowed to spread into a destructive wildfire. At the Water Base, I learned the greatest methods of combating my ego through tapping into a great spiritual unconscious. The lessons of the Earth Base taught me about the irreplaceable value of co-dependency with the planet. All of those lessons fueled each other and prepared me for my greatest lesson to date: the art and science of letting go. My experiences at 3 Lionz demonstrated the unexpected value of letting go of everything that I ever worked towards and held dear. In the short time that I lived there, there was a fairly sudden and drastic detachment from many worldly concerns. Symbolically, I carelessly left my Blackberry phone in a store and it was stolen the very first week that I moved into the house. I no longer had that database of contact information that I amassed through my professional network and there was one less way for most people to get in touch with me. I simply existed on that hill, hardly descending for trivial or even some seemingly important reasons. Everyday that I woke up, I discovered that I was immensely blessed and it was that reality that kept me alive when meals were scarce and money for rent was barely being found. I continued to do what I could for Manifesto|Jamaica while earning my income by writing for inspiring people like Don Corleon and Mykal Cushnie. I also wrote articles for the College Lifestyle magazine and started a regular column in the Aesthetics Now magazine, an undoubtedly revolutionary online publication founded by Neville Ewers and another good friend of mine, Simone Colosi (soon to be Simone Ewers), an Australian who stumbled upon IdlerzLounge.com during its earliest days and grew to become a Jamaican at heart.

To my dismay, Reggie and I could no longer afford the accommodations and I had to quickly come to terms with the fact that we would last only five months at 3 Lionz. We were only able to last that long because we had external assistance as well as a contributing houseguest – a brethren called Jacek from Canada – for a majority of the duration. It was a saddening turn of events yet I felt it coming. After all, it was quite fitting that the exact location that inspired me to practice detachment would, itself, challenge me to demonstrate my ability to accept the loss of things and circumstances that I felt I earned and deserved. I had to quickly accept the fact that 3 Lionz did what it was supposed to do for me and I was happy that I enjoyed it to the fullest.

As I treasured the final moments with my Air Base, I started to prepare myself for the end of a life chapter, one that started almost four years before. At that time, I left the United States to make the energy of my youth count towards mobilizing all the young people of my homeland. Truth be told, I was not necessarily going to witness the emphatic rise I envisioned, but at least I knew that my efforts directly translated into the mobilization of a sizeable collective of positive, energetic peers. I had to recognize that they were more likely than I to see the mission through to the end. Again, I detected another similarity between my 18th and 21st century contributions. Even though the circumstances of the revolution differed, I instinctively knew in both eras that certain others had integral roles to carry out as the revolution unfolded and that I would inevitably be removed from the battlefield. In Haiti, I was killed – beheaded by my enemies. In Jamaica, I opted for an extraction strategy that would prolong my life on Earth. In this era, I escape with breath in me, so that I can speak on my own behalf.

23
THE COCONUT

On August 13, 2010, Manifesto|Jamaica staged its first of three *ART'ical Exposure* events at Bookophilia. I was happy about having a direct hand in arranging that partnership with Andrea Dempster, who I viewed as a revolutionary businesswoman. I loved the appealing way in which books were presented at her store and I also fancied its address, 92 Hope Road, which gave me the same feeling as saying "fifty-six Hope Road" whenever I said it to myself.

ART'ical Exposure was a great experience and learning process that night, and I think that the entire team sensed that we had broken through the barrier of uncertainty. The media was fascinated by Manifesto|Jamaica and it was now going to be recognized for what it was, what we created it to be: a national beacon of hope. The mission was far from accomplished but I was beginning to feel like it was time for me to rest. I was not in the best of health, having survived on very poor dietary habits over the course of the previous months, and I had lost a lot of weight, which I didn't have much of to begin with. I was already making plans to travel to Washington, DC, where I would recuperate before the main event in October – the *Manifesto|Jamaica Festival of ART'ical Empowerment*. Waiting for me was my empress, Sasha, whose unique balance of militancy and femininity was the basis of her magnetism and the first of many reasons why I continue to love her today. I was very eager to see her but, before leaving the Rock, I decided to stay long enough to recite some words at the second *ART'ical Exposure* on August 27. It was an excerpt from a book given to me by a globetrotting, revolutionary man called Atua Dub or, simply, Dub. I was very moved by the specific words that I intended to read to the audience that evening* and I made sure to put on the Sleeve of Justice for the occasion. By then, it was very loose fitting on me, to understate the reality of what I looked like as I wore it, but I wanted people to see what somebody fighting for personal and universal liberation looked like before I claimed my revolutionary sabbatical.

Before the proceedings began, I saw Mama G, who was invited to conduct the libation. We had a serious conversation as she gathered her things in preparation and, as if she knew of my intentions to go on stage that night, she spoke some of the most empowering words into my being. That was when I knew that the Universe was in approval of what I was going to do. I later sat in the front row and watched Mama G perform the libation, spreading a potent dose of blessings for the benefit of those in attendance and for the benefit of Manifesto|Jamaica. I was particularly attracted to a coconut, which she offered to be passed around the venue so that everyone could hold it and release their stresses into it. The mystical relevance of that coconut struck me in the most profound way and I proceeded to collect it when the participating audience was done with it. I took it back to Mama G and she told me that it was mine to do with it what I willed. She suggested that it be broken when Manifesto|Jamaica needed it most, whether for money or some other stroke of good fortune. That night, I took it around to as many Manifesto|Jamaica team members as I could recognize (whoever didn't seem too busy) so that they could hold it. After *ART'ical Exposure* ended, I took the coconut with me to 3 Lionz.

---

* The video recording of this recital can be viewed at Duttyism.com

On August 30, I was on my way to Washington but not before leaving the coconut in a safe location: House of Diggy. When I returned to Kingston five weeks later, I retrieved it and resumed my meditation in search of the answer to the question, "What should I do with it?" I wanted to take it with me to the final pre-festival meeting at the Edna Manley College and break it in the presence of as many team members as possible, including the Canadian support team members who travelled to be with us, but the conditions there did not feel appropriate. Nothing indicated to me that I should break the coconut before the festival, even though I really wanted to do so. The four days of events proceeded splendidly and I even enjoyed an unexpected moment in the spotlight when Abishai (one of Taiwo's Bebble Rock comrades) asked me to be the master of ceremonies for a talent show on Saturday, October 16. On the night after that, I found myself dancing on stage as Oje performed 'Wrong Side Of The Law' at our main event. That was my victory dance.

It was not until after the festival, on the night of October 22, that I instinctively knew that I should break the coconut. The moon was full and the sky was cloudy. A light drizzle started as the sweet water spread over the concrete – the beginnings of a release of all that was held in. I did it because it was precisely in the immediate aftermath of the Festival of ART'ical Empowerment, as the team proceeded to the important phase of laying the bricks on top of the foundation, that Manifesto|Jamaica needed the added protection. I did it for all my loved ones whose stories, what I knew of them, were worthy to be told. I did it for myself so that I might find closure...

...Days later, I left Jamaica without fanfare.

TOP: During our hike to the waterfall, we pause to catch our breaths at this beach clearing.
(L-R) Doug, Foodie, Peter, Simone, Reggie, Raqs and me, looking towards the rest of the journey.
(Photographer: N/A)
BOTTOM: One of the earliest episodes of Reasoning, I am preparing to go on air. (Photographer: N/A)

TOP LEFT: Delivering my speech, 'The Way Forward for Pan-African Youth' at the Africa Unite Youth Symposium. Seated are (L-R) Donisha and Choc'late. (Photographer: N/A)
TOP RIGHT: Mama G responding to the speech. (Photographer: N/A)
BOTTOM: Paul, Lesley and I sitting on the grounds of the Bob Marley Mausoleum in Nine Mile. (Photographer: N/A)

TOP: The last Idlerz' Lounge party before I shut down the website. (L-R) Trevor, Reggie, me, Froggy, Strachan and Biggs. (Photographer: N/A)
BELOW: "Twins," Gavin and Gavin during the latter's radio show in Toronto. (Photographer: N/A)

BOTTOM LEFT: The five Regional Coordinators for Ignite The Americas. (L-R) Panmela Castro of Brazil, Jorge Salazar of Canada, Lia Samantha of Colombia, Toki Wright of the USA and Jamaica's very own... me. (Photographer: N/A)
BOTTOM RIGHT: Che and I sharing a moment of celebration after a successful Ignite The Americas. (Photographer: N/A)

TOP: Touching base with Oje in Jamaica, in between Florida trips. *(Photographer: Kaysian Wilson)* BOTTOM: AMSC - Artists Make Stuff Cool - inside Tuff Gong's recording studio before heading to Nine Mile, months before I would actually work there. (L-R) Kate standing, Mark sitting, Che standing, Mina sitting, me sitting, Tiffany standing. *(Photographer: Mina Mikhail)*

TOP: A great moment that captures our affection for the people of Nine Mile, especially these people. (*Photographer: Mina Mikhail*)
BOTTOM: The microphone and I are reunited during the first Reasoning since completing my mission in Florida. (*Photographer: Marla Hitchins*)

RIVER EXCURSIONS: (FROM TOP TO BOTTOM)
- A bottle of herb wine and the exhilarating impact of rushing cold water! (Photographer: Zina Salih)
- Meditating on a very large river rock. (Photographer: Zina Salih)
- One of my favourite things to do, hop around from stone to stone. (Photographer: Zina Salih)
- Reggie and I about to hold a medz off the airwaves. (Photographer: N/A)

TOP: Enjoying a moment with Janine and Oje. *(Photographer: Zina Salih)*
BOTTOM LEFT: Shortly before Oje's performance at The Seven Year Wish. *(Photographer: N/A)*
BOTTOM RIGHT: A legendary Manifesto | Jamaica meeting. (Clockwise from left) Neville, Gregory, Maria, Reggie, me, Kareece, Natalie (mostly hidden), Roxy (partially hidden), Abishai, Janine, Lesley. *(Photographer: Keron 'Kabaka Pyramid' Salmon)*

MANIFESTO | JAMAICA FESTIVAL MOMENTS: *(FROM TOP TO BOTTOM)*
- Me being invited on stage during Oje's performance and deciding to record him up close and personal in the process. *(Photographer: Sabriya Simon)*
- Me dancing on a stage was unheard of before that night. *(Photographer: Sabriya Simon)*

(Photographer: Sabriya Simon)

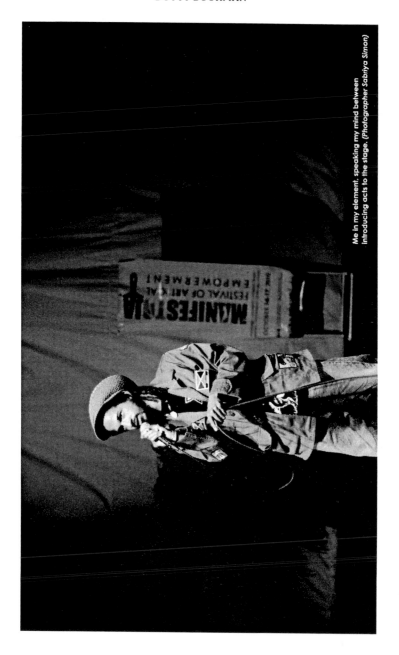

Me in my element, speaking my mind between introducing acts to the stage. *(Photographer Sabriya Simon)*

EPILOGUE

"Do you remember the man who did everything in his power to make life better for us? He was a great ancestor, wasn't he? I didn't get a chance to meet him because he passed away from the Earth so many years ago but I am grateful that he left some clues with us, so that we may continue to liberate ourselves."

So that somebody will say those words about me in the future is the reason why I have told my story and why I intend to continue writing. I owe my accomplishments to the inspiration from so many others before me who could not have inspired me unless I was able to absorb their messages and learn what they considered the important lessons of their own time. In the same way, somebody else will owe his or her accomplishments to me and we will share in the honor because we both will owe it to the will of the Universe. I accept that I am an instrument of the Universe and, therefore, I accept any credit for the successes achieved through the focus of my open mind; likewise, I accept any discredit for the failures that occurred when I was out of alignment with the natural and universal order.

If you consider yourself a revolutionary being who seeks ultimate peace and harmony on this planet, you have to work to finish the mission. If you are not in the position to finish the job, do all that you are capable of doing and then, importantly, pass on the knowledge to your children and their generation so that they will have a better chance of finishing the job. Surely, in this way, the task will be complete in due time.

With gratitude,
Dutty Bookman.

GIVING THANKS

I am thankful for Life and for being able to tread along my path proudly, sharing in knowledge, growing in humility and basking in love. In the fullness of my capacity, I recognize the active Universe and the great ancestors who continue to assist me from the realm where they exist. In particular, I praise the name and spirit of His Imperial Majesty, Haile Selassie I, the power of the trinity and my compass in these times; I praise the name and spirit of Bob Marley, who has accommodated and strengthened me in countless ways along my journey; I praise the name and spirit of Marcus Mosiah Garvey, a useful companion in the heart of the whirlwind; I praise the name and spirit of Ernesto 'Che' Guevara, who provides a great example of intellectual service to humanity. Finally, I praise the name and spirit of Dutty Boukman, whose name I am honored to carry on with pride. There are many other ancestors who have directly or indirectly influenced the quality of my existence; I praise them all.

My mother, Carrol, is a consistently patient and caring soul. I must have purposely selected her before I left the spirit realm so that she would raise me on Earth. She and I both know how impossible it is for me to repay her in this lifetime, so I will do as much as I can. My father, Glenford, has been a sporadic presence in my life, but he has a good heart and I continue to enjoy our conversations. My sister, Golda, is a great example of an individual who is very loving without overt displays of affection. She has always supported me in timely fashion. All my extended family members who I know and love are also important to me.

Empress Sasha is my healer and enabler. When I was very weak, she donated some of her own strength in order to rehabilitate me, physically and emotionally. Our spiritual similarities form the basis of our partnership and I can hardly imagine a better co-creator and mother for my offspring in these times. I automatically support her, whatever her aspirations.

Words can hardly express what my revolutionary brother, Reggie, means to me. We've been in the trenches together and it is always my honor to build with him. My respect extends to the Canteen Crew and other valued friends whose longevity of camaraderie and support in my life thus far is much appreciated. I also wish continued blessings onto Stagga, with whom I learned the important art of holding firm. The friendship and perspective of Keri Joseph is invaluable to me, and her family might as well be my own. I have gained immeasurably as I have grown in brotherhood with Oje, whose determination, presence of mind and consequent accomplishments inspire me to no end. The mystic simply cannot be taught.

I am extremely fortunate to know my friends, Simone and Neville Ewers of Aesthetics Now, and to benefit from their professional expertise. In particular, Simone endured the brunt of my persistence as I wore my editor's cap. That was probably not easy.

There are too many names in my mind when I think about IdlerzLounge.com. All of its accomplishments happened because of people power. To avoid the risk of forgetting even one name, I refrain from listing any but they all must know that I feel indebted to them. Likewise, a great pool of persons made themselves available to help with Reasoning, whether through research or by sitting on the studio panel on a Wednesday night when they clearly preferred to sleep earlier.

The energy of that phenomenal human being known as Che is beyond comprehension at times. The alignment of our respective visions, and the resulting work done together so far, has probably benefited me more than him. Reflections about the city of Toronto and the ones who I met there remind me that more positivity exists in the world than mainstream media would have me believe. I am especially happy to have come in contact with those who appropriately displayed the indomitable spirit of the indigenous peoples of the Americas.

Even though I am one of the instigators who steered Manifesto|Jamaica on its course, I am fortunate to know the industrious people who really made it happen and who are continuing the artistic revolution on that front. I am happy to be of further assistance through any means within my capacity. My pride in the organization, and the individuals who are putting the energy of their youth into it, sometimes makes me emotional.

To my friends at Tuff Gong International, Bob Marley Museum and Bob Marley Foundation, I wish many blessings. Thank you for being a part of the natural mystic that lifted my spirits so often.

I salute all my elders who are still working towards true liberation and who concern themselves with transferring their wisdoms for the continuation of the task at hand. I especially acknowledge those who I have been honored to speak with and learn from, and who touched me in memorable ways. I want to send my love and respect to John Maxwell, who recently graduated to the status of revered ancestor. As he instructed me, I will continue to disseminate the truth in my writings.

I applaud all who consciously decide to labor for reasons that encompass more than their individual aspirations, particularly the ones who do so in public view. These persons expose themselves, sometimes at great risk to their lives, privacy or sanity, to represent a positive cause; and all such causes are subsets of the one major cause of Justice, which is Truth, which is Life. The persistence of these persons is very important because they are often considered the faces of movements, and that is sometimes the extent of their purpose. The loyalty of their supporters empowers them to continue along their path; therefore, the non-faces are the real collective source of revolutionary power. People who actively defend and reinforce whatever and whoever aligns with the universal values of Justice, Truth, Life, I salute them.

I also wish to recognize the good people whose names I have mentioned in this book, or who I otherwise thought about while writing the book, or who gave me great encouragement during the whole process. A complete list can be found at my website, Duttyism.com.

THE SPEECH

The following is the written version of my speech, 'The Way Forward for Pan-African Youth.' On February 6, 2008 at Liberty Hall, I read from a printed copy resembling what is below, improvising a few moments but, for the most part, saying precisely these words. It is also important to know that the song called 'The Mission' (by Damian Marley and Stephen Marley) was purposely played on the sound system just before I began the speech. A video recording of my oral delivery is also available to be viewed at Duttyism.com.

Have a plan. Have some ambition. Make sure we are firm in the Armageddon. These are the words of Damian "Jr. Gong" Marley and the song is called "The Mission."

By now, we should all have an awareness of the complex array of problems that we face. What we need now is a collective plan, a collective ambition.

Word of Caution

White-bashing is dangerous. Some of us may have white friends who we are going to smile and laugh with after this Symposium is done. And that can be seen as hypocritical. We are rightfully cautious of Caucasians because we have history to back us up, but history also backs up the contrary. During the days of slavery in the United States for instance, there was a system for freeing slaves called the Underground Railroad. When Harriet Tubman and others were guiding slaves to free lands under the cover of night, black AND WHITE people were hiding them in their homes by day.

On the other hand, due to factors such as the Willie Lynch Syndrome, there were, and still are BLACK PEOPLE WHO ASSIST AND OTHERWISE ACCEPT the continued oppression of their fellow black brothers and sisters.

Why am I saying this? I am saying this because I believe we must be less suspicious of white people because of their skin type, and MORE AWARE of the differences between good and evil human beings. Good knows no skin barriers; good knows no religious barriers; good knows no national barriers. Likewise, evil is not restricted by any characteristic that is easy to single out without getting to know a person.

It is when you have an objective conversation with a fellow human being, that you can get a proper understanding of the good or evil – or even the neutrality - in that person. Complete objectivity may be an unrealistic ideal for most of us, especially as we have been conditioned to judge people based on initial appearances. We should, at least, give others a fair chance to prove our preconceived notions right or wrong before we pass a final judgement.

With that said, the way forward should incline us to build an army of goodness. Good people, as opposed to good warriors, or good scientists, or good businesspersons, or good politicians, should be the very foundation upon which we stand. Adolf Hitler was an excellent political leader, but was he a good person? When we unite with goodness as the common denominator, we will find that the passion, which drives us to conquer evil, will make us the greatest warriors, scientists, businesspersons and politicians this Earth has ever seen.

What We Should Aim to Achieve

With that said, what should we aim to achieve? We know of the criminality which plagues us, but you can't blame the youth. We know of the diseases running rampant in Black populations across the world. We can't blame the youth for that either.

A repetitive theme in our symposium is the need to control our economic destiny. I have been giving this some thought for a long time now, and I concluded to myself that, one, economic independence will be necessary for us to rid ourselves of these other problems. Secondly, for us to attain this kind of independence, Africans worldwide would have to recognize and pinpoint our competitive advantages in the global market. Two things immediately came to my mind: our artistic expressions and our athletic prowess.

In the arts, our western musical styles like Reggae, Dancehall and Hiphop are so widely recognized and influential, and they generate so much income, that we cannot sit down and allow the revenue to continue flowing into foreign hands. Reggae is a perfect example of something distinctively ours that is exploited by Europeans for their economic gain. This has to stop. Let us regulate our art and craft industries for the material gain of Africans. Let us teach music-related trades to our people. Teach some to be producers, develop voice training academies, offer affordable courses in artist management and publicity.

When are we going to develop our own film industry? The US has their Hollywood, or Follywood if you ask me. The Indians have their Bollywood. Let us cut our own piece of the film pie – Jollywood if you will. I know we can create our own distinctive, positive style because I have been to China and I have seen it with my own eyes.

In sports, Jamaica alone racks up athletic medals like nobody's business. When it comes to sprinting, the United States know that the Olympic gold in the 100m, the 200m, the 400m, the relays will most likely elude them if they cannot run better times than the Jamaicans. Ironically, what colour are most, if not all of the United States sprinters?

In long distance challenges, which countries dominate? Ethiopia and Kenya come to my mind immediately. This tells me something about the spirit of the continental Africans. They endure. Not only do they endure miles of running, but they endure miles of oppression. They are unbreakable. In fact, if you listen to "The Mission," you will hear Jr. Gong say, "The race is not just for the swift, but those who can endure." Well look at that: Black people are swift AND Black people are enduring. This reinforces, in me, a confidence in the victory of good over evil.

So let us build sporting academies that employ our greatest athletes as coaches, and attract and nurture our greatest young talents. Let us try to develop our own equipment - footballs, running shoes, whistles, uniforms – instead of importing from places like China. Put our people to work.

Speaking of building things, look at the aviation industry right now. Air travel has grown to never-before-seen heights. While it may seem like a lot of non-African nations stand to reap most of the economic benefit from the airline industry, have we thought about setting up factories that can make simple components like the nuts and bolts that hold the plane together? It's not that I know the specifics involved in getting this kind of thing done; it's not that I know whether or not we would have the resources or the competitive advantage to profit; my point is that we have to think outside of the box. If it so happened that we COULD comfortably and profitably develop these simple but essential parts of an airplane, then think about how many nuts and bolts on a SINGLE aircraft. Then multiple that by the quantity of aircrafts that are being developed and built constantly on a day to day basis; and this is in one of the hottest industries of our times. This could be another way for us to benefit from tourism.

Another possibility to explore is the legalization of marijuana. Dr. Chevannes, who spoke yesterday, has been on my programme to discuss this, and he is a much greater wealth of information on the subject than I am, but here are my thoughts. If we can consume tobacco cigarettes that are deliberately made with harmful and addictive chemicals, and have in bold print "Smoking kills" on the package, then we sure as hell can smoke some natural herbs freely in the streets. The USA has its "medical marijuana." In other words, they are rubbing it in our face that they can do as they please as they pressure us, in places like Jamaica, to refrain from exploiting our own abundant natural resource. Nonsense! We must legalize it, smoke it and build a textile industry around it. In Jamaica, the buzz phrase of today is "Brand Jamaica," so how comes we don't make cannabis clothing lines? There are countries we can trade with; we can trade among ourselves. If the creators of the so-called "War on Drugs" don't like it, tell them to come and do something about it! We have the warriors to face them. Let them come and give our young shottas a common enemy. The gangsters have blood in their eyes, and I assure you, if they see self-preservation in progress, I dare any foreign entity to try and stop us.

Lastly, and most dear to my heart, we must aim for the ideal of responsible Black media. Mutabaruka said it all, and there isn't much more that I can add. I will say this: I am often terrified of public speaking, but when I was given the chance to pilot my own radio talk show, and having a long-standing disgust with the state of the media in these times, I could not refuse the opportunity. Sometimes your destiny grabs you, ready or not.

Let us hold our media personalities and our media houses responsible. I have always made it clear on my show that I am open to constructive criticism, and today I say to you, my friends, guide us media people in times of obvious ignorance, and scold us harshly when we blatantly contribute to the downgrading of our society. We are rebuilding a nation – the Black nation. This is serious business.

Let us try to understand the perspective of U.S. and European based Blacks who are living in lands governed by white establishments. Let us try to understand the plight of the small, developing, and frankly dependent Black nations of the West Indies. Let us try to understand the reality of a struggling continental Africa. Our different perspectives should not be a dividing factor, but rather a unifying factor. We each bring a different dish to the table that, when compiled with the other dishes, will make a savoury 3-course meal of liberation for our people. We can do it.

Individual Development

In closing, allow me to stress the importance of the individual in this collective experience. Each of us is an ingredient in the specific dish that we are preparing. Too many cooks spoil the broth they say. In my opinion, we need as many cooks as we can get, but each cook's ingredient must be of the best quality. When cooking curry chicken, we want the best curry, the best pieces of chicken, the best pot, and so on. Likewise, we need each human ingredient in our liberation struggle to be the best he or she can be. This can only be done through self-development, by seeking knowledge. Once we seek the truth, we will be inevitable victorious. My personal mantra is "Knowledge. Humility. Love." Let me explain.

Recall the theme song again. Marcus Garvey said to read. Knowledge is the key. I know that this is true from my own life experience. I am not afraid to admit to anyone that I am coming from a state of complete ignorance. My ignorance still exists in many ways today, but each and every time I pick up a book, complete it and put it down, I feel more empowered with my next breath. It does not even matter much what the subject matter of the book is, and, if not a book, I will do my own reading on the internet.

Knowledge is power.

As a person who did not enjoy reading in my teenage years, the first book I willingly read in my early twenties was a biography of Che Guevara called Che Guevara: A Revolutionary Life. I picked it up because I wanted to know why this guy's face was on so many t-shirts (note: in this context, t-shirts could fall into the category of MEDIA). After I read it, I came to learn of this South American-born, Cuban revolutionary liberator and my life was transformed; and so, a chronic book-reading habit began. And the more I read, the more powerful I felt; the more confident I felt.

With this confidence, one may easily fall into the trap of boasting or hyping up oneself with the newfound consciousness. I was very close at times, but I eventually came to the realization that the effect of knowledge on a truly open mind is to show you yourself and, in doing so, show you that you know nothing at all. Ironic as it seemed, the more I knew was the more I realized how little I knew. In fact, I became so embarrassed within myself that I had no choice but to be humble.

Humility over hype.

When I got to the inevitable point of humility, I had to stop and think, "What now?"

Now that I could see myself better than any mirror could reflect my image, I was forced to acknowledge my strengths and weaknesses, and I had to recognize, very quickly, that my survival in the Armageddon will require the assistance of others whose strengths pick up where my weaknesses fall short.

So, teamwork is necessary right?

So with teamwork being necessary, with teamwork being a prerequisite to our collective survival in the midst of oppression, we must consider the best way to approach the concept of a team. We can simply choose to use each other's strengths as a means to an end, our own end, and in this process we have no idea who we're working with. Or we can choose to build relationships underlined with goodness, and understand our commonalities and work towards them. I, for one, prefer the latter option, and there is absolutely no other way to do this than through UNIVERSAL LOVE, or should I say INIVERSAL LOVE...

Ziggy Marley's hit song says it best – Love is my religion.

With that said, my fellow humans, let us invoke the words of the great Bob Marley, on this his

Earthday, and live in love. One Love. One Heart.
Let's get together and feel alright. Africa Unite.

Give thanks.

THE SHORT STORIES

These are the "ammo" – the three short stories that I wrote in 2009. After some private distribution, I decided to put them online for public consumption. The response was overwhelmingly positive, so much so that I was heavily considering writing my first book as a work of fiction based on the same facts in this publication ('Tried & True'). In the end, I decided against talking about myself in the third person, giving myself the aura of a hero figure and, in the process, increasing the probability of people confusing the seriousness of my story with entertainment. Even so, I remain open to doing similar short stories in the future because they are effective and there are abundant experiences to convert into stories.

#1 – Spot Check

Dutty once found himself on the wrong side of the law. He had only just left the Fire Base, where he finally utilized the chalice he received weeks earlier as a gift, and was on his way back to his abode when the Dragon caught him off guard. This time, it manifested in the form of a spot check by the Jamaica Constabulary Force. He was charged for possession of fifty dollars – JMD - worth of marijuana as well as the chalice. Both items, illegal according to the nation's colonially crafted law books, were confiscated by the officers who were inclined to let Dutty go charge-free but for the strict supervision technique displayed by the khaki-wearing inspector, one of the Dragon's favourite manifestations since it facilitated more of its damaging tendencies.

"Listen squadie, just mek sure seh you gimme a Tuesday or a Wednesday, zeen," Dutty matter-of-factly told #11747 inside the station, "Mi can make it on any of those two days but no courtroom naa see me any other day of the week, can tell you dat."

He quickly returned his attention to #9490 whom he was engaging in a moderately thought-provoking discussion.

"One thing though, boss. Corruption deh pon both side of this t'ing."

The officer nodded nonchalantly in agreement.

"Badman out ah road disguised as innocent people, zeen," a short pause accommodated a more assertive nod, "And badman deh inna the force as your colleague dem, disguised as officers of the law."

"Yes, of course." A 'what's the moral of your story?' look was on #9490's face. Dutty was just about to turn up the intensity of the discussion when he was interrupted by #11747... again.

"Listen, I'm giving you the twenty-first and..."
"Twenty-first of?"
"April, and..."

"Iz a Tuesday or a Wednesday, right?" Dutty was openly impatient with this constant human-based intrusion into his more psychoanalytically stimulating conversation.

"Yes, a Tuesday."
"Okay, and wha' else you were saying now?"
"Oh, and you will be required to pay these fines. One thousand for the herbs and one thousand for the chillum pipe."
"And I goin' get back my chalice, right?."
"Yuh wah?"
"The chillum pipe, sah." There was no response to the question. Dutty momentarily wondered if the squadie was even Jamaican.

"Sign here and here," #11747 continued, "And here, here, and here."

The inspector, feeling powerful in his close-fitting khaki uniform, walked bossily into the booking area and stood next to Dutty just as he was putting the finishing touches on the final dotted line.

"You want back the weed, eh?" The Dragon was clearly using this soul for maximum provocation. Dutty was quite peeved that men could fail so badly at guarding their very essence from such contamination; he relented nevertheless.

"No man, everyt'ing criss," Dutty retorted, "But you can gimme back the chalice when you ready still."

#2 – Judge Judy

International Ganja Day came and went without a single speck of marijuana smoke entering Dutty's lunges. Close to half a decade, it must have been, since he could even think the thought of not smoking on the twentieth day of April. A practicing herbalist, and an avid reader as well, he was a little more than competent at feeding his brain.

The following day, April twenty-first, he arose to absorb his share of the spirit of Haile Selassie I. It was exactly forty-three years to the date since the famed emperor of Ethiopia brought sunshine with him on a rainy Kingston day.

Hold on deh - an alarming and timely recollection surfaced in Dutty's mind - *April twenty-one... that is my court date!*

Indeed, it was Tuesday. Dutty had made a point of requesting a Tuesday or a Wednesday to pay his fines and the booking officer was kind enough to grant the request. Suddenly, the appointment was transported from the future to the present. There was no time indicated on the paper given to him when he was charged but, assured that the universe would have him arrive at the courthouse at the right time, he went casually about his morning ritual. Following a relaxing shower, he felt the urge to get dressed immediately even though he had no intention of leaving home quite yet. After putting on his clothes, he observed his arms automatically lacing up his Gideon Boots.

Well then, I guess I'm about to step out the door.

Dutty stepped out the door with that thought. With little hesitation, he was on the boulevard buying a jelly coconut. After his potassium intake, he went directly to the courthouse, finding the courtroom with surprising ease. He walked in, followed closely by two other inconvenienced citizens of Jamaica just before the doors were pulled shut. All subsequent individuals were prohibited from entry. Dutty checked his watch, realizing it was precisely ten-o-clock.

"I guess court starts at ten then," he mumbled to himself.

The universe definitely wanted him to be on time. The Dragon's aura had effortlessly penetrated the roughly one hundred earthlings in the room. Fifty or so gathered jovially on one side, including judge, lawyers and red and blue seamed police officers. Fifty or so ordinary citizens were on the other side, Dutty's side, preoccupied with feelings of fear, anxiety and depression associated with the various charges against them. So consumed they were that they didn't notice that they had front row tickets to one of Jamaica's most notorious poppy shows – its justice system. On the other hand, Dutty was more than ready to enjoy the proceedings.

It was immediately and painfully obvious from the onset that the childish group had a certain routine for ridiculing the worried bunch. A specific lawyer, sitting as an observer, seemingly served to play the role of heckler; at random intervals he would shout demands at the standing accused of the moment. With mimicking echoes from two of the police officers in the room, Dutty heard statements that made him cringe a little.

"Put your hands at your sides!"

"Beg for mercy bwoy!"

"Call her *Your Honour*! Who yuh t'ink you talking to?!"

"Rasta bwoy, yuh want me cut off yuh locks!"

Invariably, these commands were closely followed by smirks of self-satisfaction. The judge would periodically ask the man to be silent; this seemed to be one of her many roles in the comedic fiasco. As for her, she was not only a judge by profession but also a self-appointed spiritual guru. For as many of the accused as she could, she concluded their cases with what she must have thought were useful bits of advice to be applied to their lives. Remembering that the Dragon constantly comforted itself with conceit, Dutty felt pity for the judge and her minions whose earthly personas were merely symptoms of its presence. He wondered what the Dragon had in store for him.

"Your name is..." the judge waited for the proper noun that would complete her sentence.
"Bookman."
"What Bookman?"
"Dutty."

She found his name on her little list and the charges were read out loud by one of her lackeys. Your Honour then asked the same question she had asked dozens of times already for the morning.

"These are the charges against you. Guilty or not guilty?"

Dutty certainly did not feel any guilt for having a spliff's worth of marijuana and an apparatus made from calabash, which grows on trees, and a plastic hose that was surely produced by the Babylonians themselves. The leaf image on the front of his shirt must have assured the judge of that. He considered the language and the implications before opening his mouth.

"Accurate," he kept a straight face.

This was not the response that Your Honour sought. The Dragon found a perfect opportunity to flex its muscles. The judge issued her warning.

"This is not a joke, young man. Are you aware that you can be put behind bars for these offenses?!"

The Dragon very well knew that when Dutty was charged days earlier, he was informed only about paying fines at the courthouse. Nobody mentioned potential jail time. In that moment, Dutty remembered the Dragon's blueprint. He had a chance to see it before. A major part of its strategy was to set up the Babylonian system to confuse the humans. Once the humans were confused, then, being that they were supposed to be the most intelligent of Earth's species and, therefore, be responsible for the upkeep of Earth, the planet was sure to implode in due time. The Dragon wanted nothing less than total destruction, the polar opposite of Creation. Trickery was its primary weapon.

Here was a prime example of why Dutty was certain that Jamaica's justice system was working for the Dragon. The police had conveniently misinformed him about the implications of his charges so that he would be surprised in court. Maintaining his composure was key.

"I actually had no idea... Your Honour."

"Well now you know," her posture relaxed as she felt in control again, "Tell me why I should not give you six months in jail."

A key part of this sitcom of law was the begging part. The creature in the dress rather enjoyed her daily dose of cracked voices and tears. A typical response was something like, *"Beg you, do, Your Honour! I have six pickney fi feed and send go to school. Mi work two job and dem goin' fire me if me end up inna jail! It won't happen again, Your Honour! Pleeeease have mercy!"*

Conversely, Dutty had no sob story. He had no offspring that he was aware of, nor did he have any job except one: to contain the Dragon until it was time to slay the Dragon. Any activity for the purpose of generating financial income was only that and nothing else. His real duty was to carry out the mission for which he was stationed on the planet. His left shoulder involuntarily shrugged as he opened his mouth to respond. He could sense that he had a lofty facial expression to match the impolite posture that his body was displaying.

"To tell you the truth, I just don't think it's a necessary reaction for fifty dollars worth of ganja and a harmless pipe."

The judge exploded, "Listen man, stop ridiculing this court!"

She turned to a blue seam, "Lock him up! He needs some time to think about it."

Of course, a chorus of chuckles hummed on that side of the room. In the lockup, there was a businessman being charged for some type of corporate fraud or the other, sitting in his fancy business suit. He whispered a word of advice as soon as Dutty entered, "When you go back out there, just tell the judge that you made an error in judgement in having the weed and the chalice. Don't let her get upset again."

Dutty nodded, "Respec'." He recognized the communication pattern of Selassie I reaching him through this man.

It was a little less than half an hour when Dutty was recalled to address the charges. He guessed it was supposedly enough time for the average fear-stricken victim of the justice system to reconsider his or her mannerism.

"Let's try this again Mr. Bookman... guilty or not guilty?"

"Guilty, I suppose," still subtly defiant with his sarcastic tone.

"Seems you have not learnt anything in there," she pointed in the direction of the lockup. It was obviously time to beat the Dragon at its silly game.

"Actually," Dutty began, "I did realize something and I would like to apologize for disrespecting the court and you. It was unintentional and I apologize." Saying *apologize* twice in the same statement was sure to disarm the judge. As expected, she glanced at her colleagues with pride as if she had just given them a live demonstration of a textbook courtroom disciplinary technique.

Meanwhile, having kept calm and void of fear, Dutty realized that he would not have been jailed for a first offence unless he grossly antagonized the judge. He was eventually dismissed with twenty-one thousand dollars in fines. Having lost the battle, the Dragon sought to humiliate Dutty before allowing him to leave the courtroom.

"You know, Mr. Bookman," it was story time again as Your Honour put her pen down and removed her glasses, "I know all about you and what you're about."

"Really, Your Honour?"

"Yes, I used to be all about black power and those things when I was a young girl. In fact, I used to wrap my hair and such."

"Oh, wow," Dutty maintained the face of an adolescent engrossed in a grandparent's recollection of the good old days.

"Then one day, my mother gave me twenty dollars. You see, that was a lot of money in my time..."

"Oh, I see," his face remained unchanged.

"...and she told me, 'Judz, go to the shop and buy some hair relaxer and some nail polish.'"

"Okay." There was a pause during which time Dutty wondered what his lesson was going to be.

"Then she said to me... and I will never forget this valuable lesson..."

Suspense was at its heights. She continued.

"'If you *look* like a hooligan, you will start
to *behave* like a hooligan, and you will eventually
become a hooligan.' You see what I'm trying to
say here?"

"Oh definitely, Your Honour, and I thank you for
your wise words." Dutty laughed to himself as he
was escorted to the processing area.

#3 – Jail Cell

For roughly ten minutes, Dutty was in a real jail
cell. Not the cozier, well-lit lockup adjoining the
courtroom upstairs, but the hard, cold and dark
dungeon downstairs where people are kept for
longer periods of time. The procedure for paying
fines apparently included locking the charged
person in such a cell until the receipt found its
way to the processing area. Furthermore, the
policewoman who escorted him out of the
courtroom told Dutty that he was not allowed to
pay the fines himself. He found it a ridiculous
notion that he would have to summon someone
during working hours for the mere purpose of
handing over some of Babylon's filthy money to a
cashier. The system left much to be desired. In
such a situation, Dutty knew well that he had to
appeal to the general compassion in the soul of

the average Jamaican – in this case, the officer - in order to combat any foothold the Dragon had in their being. He reasoned with the officer, therefore, until she decided to do him a favour. He gave her one Sangster and two Manley bills, trusting that she would not pocket them for herself, then went into the indicated cell where three other young men were already incarcerated. He was happy not to be squeezed inside the cell next to it, which was filled with an indeterminably large number of young men; so many that arms were outstretched through the bars. The businessman who advised Dutty just minutes before in the courtroom lockup area was being ushered into an empty cell where he would remain by himself.

Of course, he's a businessman and not the scourge of society like us hooligans in here, Dutty thought to himself. He took out his book - the same one that he was reading in the courtroom until an officer told him to put it away - and continued his day's feeding of knowledge. Five minutes into his reading, the cell gate opened and a fifth occupant stepped inside. A talkative fellow, standing closest to the gate, turned to the newcomer after the officer walked off.

"How much you get?"

The new cellmate let out a hiss, "Five bills."

"Oh, yuh lucky. T'ree grand me get," the first responded, "And him get two t'ousand, one hundrid." He was pointing at Dutty who decided

just then to rest his eyes in the poor light. Closing
the book, he looked around the cell. The seating
was a concrete extension of the wall opposite the
entrance, bringing back memories of his days in
high school. He was at one end, his back to the
corner as was his usual style. Two other silent
men were sitting as well, one with his back to the
other corner, the other about halfway between
them, but closer to Dutty. The walls were
adorned with the scribbling of past inmates who
vowed revenge on the system and its various
proponents, whether the police, the judges and
lawyers, or the informers whose efficient
reporting led them to their present location.

When me come out, me just go get a new gun,
was one declaration written with a blue marker,
except there was an actual drawing of a handgun
in place of the word *gun*. Dutty thought that it
could have been more artistic, first of all, and,
furthermore, he lamented at the ineffectiveness
of the justice system at reforming and
reintegrating the nation's misguided youth.

"Bookman! Is there a Bookman here!" A voice
shouted down the corridor. It seemed as though
the lady actually paid the fine for Dutty.

"Yeah," he responded calmly yet audibly.

"Where?" The voice was closer.

"In here."

One male officer opened the gate as Dutty slowly

put his book in his bag. The loudmouthed cellmate, eager to be freed himself, addressed Dutty excitedly.

"Come yout', wha' yuh ah do? Read book? Your turn, man!"

On the way out, he silently blessed the officer who paid the fine for him and left the building. Half an hour later, he found himself wondering why the Dragon would have allowed him to get so deep inside its facilities just to release him.

"Oh well," he sighed to himself, simultaneously blowing smoke into the atmosphere.